MAN AND HIS DEEDS

MAN

AND HIS

DEEDS

by

Manès Sperber

Translated from the French and the

German by Joachim Neugroschel

McGRAW-HILL BOOK COMPANY

New York   St. Louis   San Francisco   Mexico

Panama   Dusseldorf   London   Sydney   Toronto

MAN AND HIS DEEDS

Library of Congress Catalog Card Number: 76-116671

First Edition

60233

CONTENTS

PREFACE

THE word *history* refers to either a series of events or their methodical presentation which permits us to grasp the causes and reasons for actions and events within their proper contexts. One lives history in the first sense of the word, one writes it in the second sense. We know who writes history. But who makes history? And who doesn't?

Monsieur Jourdain, Molière's comical *bourgeois gentilhomme,* is vastly surprised to discover that he has been speaking prose all his life. Likewise, the individual discovers in times of religious, political, or social conflict that he is virtually locked up in a period of history, willy-nilly, that he really no longer belongs to himself or his family but to a "greater collectivity," and that he has been called upon to participate in the realization of world-historic events, in service either to the nation or some movement: he may have to conquer hostile nations or parties, replace one system with another, insure a sublime future, and thus both set an example for the world and force an ultimate cure upon it.

It is only when these long holidays from everyday life begin that each man realizes that, although previously unaware of it, he has always been right in the midst of things. But he forgets, as soon as order—any order—is restored and everyday life has become omnipotent again.

History is permanent. The outbreak of any catastrophe is not a beginning but the end of a protracted, multiple process, usually unfolding in full view yet nevertheless misunderstood, misinterpreted, and misjudged. Who can say that from the very start he has always accurately judged the results and significance of every important encounter, relationship, or action? Who among us hasn't made a mistake, or been disappointed? And yet the factors that have to be taken into account in every personal decision are trivial in comparison with those determining the life of a group. But even a precise distinction between conditional and determining factors is at times so difficult that the probability of error is nearly as great as that of sufficient insight.

Hardly a generation has actually shaped history the way it intended to; none has really accomplished what it thought it would. Each has failed to realize that its victories would sooner or later lead to effects that would vitiate success and triumph and virtually invalidate them.

It was fifty years ago at the latest, during World War I, that the inhabitants of our planet were thrust by the history of their countries from countless local histories into world history. Since then, every event, no matter where it has occurred, has been capable of assuming worldwide scope: Danzig is, so to speak, everywhere; any local conflict can become universal simply because local history is no longer isolatable. In our age, world history has become destiny—a daily event concerning even the man who closes his eyes to it. This state of affairs is not plain and evident to most people even when they do not expressly question it. Nor have radio, television, nuclear fission, or space travel changed matters any: a false awareness of history is a characteristic product of the century that began on August 1, 1914, and has, ever since, been continuously producing homicidal myths and mass-murderous legends.

Each era discovers and invents for its own use a past best fitted to its conception of the future. Human history has tidings only for those who await them and anticipate their contents. Man discovers the secrets whose solution he already knows; man discovers the lock for which he has a key in his pocket.

The author of the essays gathered in this volume is fully aware of this, which is why he rarely or never forgets to expose himself to his own skepticism even in the midst of writing. Thus he always remains conscious of the fact that there are other locks besides the one which his key fits.

At first sight, this statement may seem questionable to the reader, since I take a decided position on every problem brought up. In point of fact, I have renounced, from my earliest days, the comfort and the many advantages accruing from a neutral position; even at the age of sixty, I cannot manage to remain indifferent or stoical. To come right out with it: I have always fought a cold war, perhaps partially because I experienced hot war as a child. In my enthusiasm for a cause, I have often taken the wrong course, but never the wrong choice of the evil that had to be fought. Common sense dictates coexistence, i.e., a peaceful parallel life of countries and peoples, even though their governments may be different or even antithetical. But common sense and decency also dictate that all men who wish to affect the awareness and the public opinion of their contemporaries without demanding any power for themselves—i.e., that intellectuals wage a cold war against everything they regard as evil—do so without any consideration for tact, tactics, or anything else.

Truth in human matters is as complex as human nature; and neither one nor the other can be simplified. Both are best expressed in fractions rather than whole numbers. Compared with them, evil is amazingly simple: concentration camps, the persecution of dissenters, the deprivation of the rights of any minorities, the suppression of political opposition, exploitation no matter how or for whose benefit—all this is villainous; and it is all the more despicable the loftier the ideals or goals it may invoke.

If I were to head this volume with a motto, it would be the following: *Against* the swivel-eyed of all religions, nations, and parties—*for* their victims, for *all* victims.

Manès Sperber

Paris

MAN AND HIS DEEDS

Pilgrims to Utopia

$\approx\approx\approx\approx\approx\approx\approx\approx\approx\approx\approx\approx\approx\approx\approx\approx\approx\approx\approx$

ACCORDING to an ancient myth found in almost every continent, world history began with an end—the end of paradise, from which the first human beings are expelled for losing their innocence; as exiles in ephemeral time, they take up the fight against hunger and death, the struggle for love and happiness.

And history proves at least one thing: that the descendants of those exiles have been trying by hook or by crook to discover the secret entrance leading back into paradise.

Whether we realize it or not, we are all migrating back to a lost paradise; no one knows the location but everyone knows for sure that it's somewhere else, far away. This knowledge gives rise to a nostalgic wanderlust at times stronger than homesickness. And a yearning for paradise includes both wanderlust *and* homesickness, a longing for vanished childhood, lost youth, the fire of burnt-out passions.

Anything lost in time, or undiscoverable, we tend to seek in a remote place, in Utopia: a "Nowhere Land." The travelers to Utopia, pilgrims to a lost paradise that must exist in Nowhere Land, keep on producing exact and meticulous descriptions—of the landscape, the equitable institutions, and the unassailable and unephemeral happiness of the people.

I

Yet innumerable authors of these realistically imaginative accounts constantly forgot themselves—so to speak—and came up with a satirical delineation of an anti-Paradise. Behind the portrayal of things as they should be, of Utopia come true, they projected, in aggressive lucidity, things as they are with all the abominable characteristics. More's *Utopia,* Swift's *Gulliver,* and all other such works offer a caricature of actual conditions that must seem all the more unbearable when confronted with the ideal and the ostensible reality of a grand and perfect world.

There have always been travel books, devoured by readers who, without leaving their armchairs, overcome all the hardships and dangers of a voyage to share the pleasure offered by exciting discoveries. These books both satisfied wanderlust and yet increased the exhilarating awareness that somewhere, beyond the farthest mountains, there must exist a world in which the sun never sets and death is conquered for all time.

For a child, every voyage—real or imaginary—is full of promise. Somewhat older, he will seek out astrologers and fortunetellers who will predict a journey (as they do for every hunter of happiness). This promise of a change of scene is virtually an announcement of imminent solution or salvation. And it is not surprising that in most narrative writing, especially in those works that one might regard as models of literary form, the central theme is often a journey taken by the hero. The change of scene, involuntary—as in the case of the infant Oedipus or young Joseph—or else desired and prepared for, always leads to an almost uninterrupted chain of encounters, experiences, and adventures. This applies to the Homeric heroes as well as to Don Quixote or Robinson Crusoe; and the voyager, a traveler to Utopia, is more frequent in our century than ever before. I mean the pilgrim who sets out to prove that his ideology and his political conception are entirely justified. He is seeking a reality: the blissful materialization of his ideal.

Since this last remark may sound ironical, I have to admit that I myself was once such a pilgrim. Way, way back. Thirty-five years ago, I visited the Soviet Union to take part in an international congress of psychologists. I was much more interested, however, in traveling around the country, to Leningrad and Kiev, Moscow and Kharkov, the Dnieprostroi, and seeing collective farms and village schools. I wanted to find some tangible confirmation that the October Revolution had created a new social order, the only equitable one, and that Russia was now in the process of producing a *new human being*. At the age of twenty-five, I was no more naive than I am today, nor less attentive or less zealous for truth. But what characterized me at the time is probably typical of any traveler to Utopia: I had set out to seek whatever would confirm my convictions and "objectively" justify my enthusiasm. A traveler of this kind may sincerely believe that he wants to discover truth; yet he is incessantly plagued by the sort of illusion he can never escape, because he creates it himself. And he creates it because he needs it, just as the deceived lover needs the delusion that he is loved and from which he concludes—appearances notwithstanding—that he simply *cannot* be deceived.

To cite an example of far more recent vintage: The well-known French writer Simone de Beauvoir, author of numerous travelogues, describes her Chinese adventures in *China*. At the very beginning of her book she tells about the lady novelist assigned to her for the trip from Mukden to Canton, a journey of several weeks. The two writers slept in the same room—and were hardly ever separated. Madame de Beauvoir, who loves to generalize, writes about Madame Sheng:

"She was, for me, a typical example of both the Chinese intellectual and the Chinese woman of her generation.

Keenly intelligent, extremely cultivated, and remarkably observant, she furnished me with invaluable information on all sorts of topics. No word of propaganda ever crossed her lips; she was far too convinced of the benefits and the necessity of the regime to toy with truth ..."

This incredible observation—whose absurd naïveté would have been scornfully attacked by Simone de Beauvoir if uttered by a rightist colleague about a Francoist traveling companion in Spain—is characteristic of the unfaltering self-delusion of such pilgrims. They would sooner believe that a camel can pass through a needle's eye than that Madame Sheng could be a specialized propaganda agent.

Nine years after Madame de Beauvoir, another French writer traveled through China, and it was his book that prompted these reflections. The title is *Journey through China* (Harper, 1966) and the author of this singular account is Jules Roy. Like his friend the unforgettable Albert Camus, Roy is a so-called *pied noir* ("black foot"), a Frenchman born and bred in Algeria. The son of poor parents, he chose a military career and became an officer. During World War II, he commanded a Royal Air Force squadron, which bombed the Ruhr for several months. His first noteworthy book, *La Vallée heureuse* (1946), was an impressive and poignant account of these flights and bombings. The book contains no sign of hostility, not even the tiniest trace of rancor toward the enemy, no cry of triumph over the destruction, no holier-than-thou attitude, and no self-complacency. Jules Roy mainly expressed his conviction that both the attackers and the attacked, the pilots in the sky and the inhabitants of the bombed cities, had been the lamentable heroes of a tragedy that had unfolded mechanically despite the power of chance. With irony and self-sarcasm, the aviators nicknamed the Ruhr Basin "the Happy Valley"; and they could just as readily have dubbed themselves the "blissful air acrobats," for they suffered from the realization that they were the agents and victims of a terrible and permanent disaster.

Thus it was that during and because of the war, Jules Roy became a writer; and although he remained an active officer in peacetime, he kept on writing and publishing. When he eventually resigned from the military, it was not because of any interference with his literary career, but because he had entered into an acrid conflict over the war in Indo-China with the French government and the leaders of the army. Out of protest, he retired prematurely as a colonel.

Next, in a series of novels, he treated the military and moral problems of those years, meeting of course with violent opposition. Moreover, he was not to succeed in truly capturing the tragically belated and totally meaningless colonial war in his narratives. It was only when he made up his mind to deal with the war in Indo-China in a huge chronicle and expose in detail the causes of the crucial defeat at Dienbienphu that he achieved the success which had been eluding him for a decade. The voluminous opus bluntly told the French the whole truth about the causes and background of their policies and strategies in Indo-China, and Jules Roy courageously came out in favor of independence for Muslim Algeria.

The author, starting out as a political liberal and a hazy leftist, was pushed more and more toward the extreme left by the influence of his own writings and their far-reaching effect. He was thus induced to play for high stakes: after exposing and fighting against his own world—the world of the *pieds noirs* and their war policy in Algeria, the military world in which he had served—he decided to write a positive book. He wanted to depict a country whose government he could laud, whose politics he could affirm and present as a glowing example. He resolved to go on a pilgrimage to China.

> I had prepared for this trip conscientiously. For six months, with the help of a sinologist, I perused the main works that had been published on China within the last century. I noted the most original observations. I studied history, society, mores, geography, philosophical and religious thought, the imperial rule, the Kuomintang, and the Communist Party. Using index cards, I registered all the events that had provoked the revolution and drew up a detailed chronology. I labored over the works of Mao Tse-tung, Confucius, and Sun Tze. I analyzed the biographies of important figures.... By the time I left for China, the files of my notes were nearly two feet high.

After protracted negotiations to procure the approval and support of the Chinese authorities, Jules Roy went to China via Russia. He intended to make a historical movie glorifying the Chinese Revolution and the Long March of Mao Tse-tung's army, and in addition write a long piece on their exemplary conquests.

Hardly a week goes by without some new book appearing on Mao's China. The authors usually haven't the vaguest notion about China's millennia-long past; and naturally they can neither speak nor even read the language. Furthermore, as their accounts reveal, these authors—with very few exceptions—were obviously all taken to the same factories, schools, model prisons, villages, popular communes, and people's museums. Even their guides, although not always the same, seem to have been interchangeably alike.

For the most part, the true pilgrims to China write enthusiastically about everything they were shown and explained. The other travelers, who arrive in a critical frame of mind, remain critical throughout their journey across the giant land and return home even more critical. Thus, one frequently feels that both types of traveler could as easily have stayed at home and spared themselves the trouble. As Pascal put it, each man looked only for whatever he had already found beforehand. Almost none was able or willing to discover anything new or perhaps contradictory.

The traveler who comes to France, England, or Germany doesn't have to overcome any obstacle between himself and naked reality. All doors are open to the man who really wants to delve beyond the surface. No one can claim that this holds for dictatorships. In Mao Tse-tung's China, you can only see what you are shown. And yet the enthusiastic pilgrims agree in advance to any limitation on their freedom of movement, proclaiming that such measures are necessary for defense against espionage, et cetera. Even reporters who bear no great love for the regime ultimately put up with these conducted tours—albeit only for professional reasons.

But to get back to the strange case of Jules Roy. What is strange about him? What is peculiar about his Chinese travel book? Well, in a certain sense the book reverses the Biblical legend of Balaam. The French writer set out to praise and to bless, but hardly a page of his book passes without his criticizing, fault-finding, grumbling, and ultimately condemning. Actually, this attitude is apparent from the very first, when he meets with Communist historians in Moscow. He asks them to clarify the Soviet position on China's Communist Party up to the victory of 1949. Jules Roy discovers that he doesn't care for these Russians, and that he likes neither Moscow, nor his hotel, nor the service.

This indicates the regrettable and highly detrimental weakness of the author and his book: for reasons that have little or nothing to do with Russia or China, he goes on his trip of many months in a grumpy and hypersensitive mood which makes him overaware of every failing and insufficiency and perhaps blind to anything positive.

The reasons? One of them, which Jules Roy presents with touching frankness, is a singular one: the middle-aged man was traveling with a very young woman whom he looked upon as his future life companion. This is why he brought her along. She was a photographer, at the start of her career. Yet the trip did not bring them any closer together. The further they got from France and the deeper their disappointment at what they saw, the more this unmatched couple grew estranged from each other. One may find the ampleness with which Jules Roy keeps on speaking about his sentimental experience and his abortive love superfluous and out of place. Yet, on the other hand, one can also admire it. As a reader and writer, and also as a critical psychologist, I tend to find it estimable of Jules Roy to be so straightforward about the elements of his subjectivity.

Be that as it may, the fact remains that the painful awareness of being disappointed in his companion or having expected the impossible of her made him suspicious of everything and everybody and, not infrequently, even spiteful.

A second reason for his, shall we say, subjective negativity is connected to another likewise frustrated expectation: the Chinese diplomatic representatives in Paris as well as certain European supporters and agents of Mao Tse-tung had led the writer to hope that he would be welcomed everywhere with open arms and in honor and receive complete assistance for all his projects. He particularly took for granted that as a trustworthy friend and admirer of the Revolution he would enjoy unlimited freedom of movement and be allowed to see and to photograph whatever he wanted to. But things worked out differently.

First, however, an observation pertaining to all intellectual pilgrims to Utopia.

All dictators, big and little, are uninterruptedly starved for flattery and adulation. Every single day, every hour, has to bring them both a full ration of worship and, as a counterpart, the vilification of their opponents. Everyone knows this. Yet few people are aware that those who serve the regime and those who wield the power are themselves extravagant flatterers, even with foreigners and especially with these strange pilgrims. Hardly a visitor to Stalin's Russia managed to resist the flattery that was laid on thick wherever one went. Today, for a start, the traveler is usually publicly lauded not merely in his own person but as an allegedly outstanding representative of his nation, his class, his profession. Children clutching flowers in their tiny fists rush in on him, look guilelessly into his eyes, and ask affectionately but insistently: "When are you going to have a revolution in your country?" Radio announcers present him to their listeners as an important personality and ask him to tell about his impressions. Naturally he only says good things, excellent things. What else could he do?

To get back to our traveler to China, Jules Roy: The people welcoming him were not as important as he had been led to believe in Paris. He was disappointed, and admits as much with the naive lack of humor which is characteristic of him and of which he is fully aware. He sensed quite correctly that, upon his arrival at Peking's airport, the absence of political V.I.P.'s could mean a dearth of interest in helping him with his movie project. And with such assistance lacking, it was naturally impossible to document the most important stages of the Long March and to present the legendary and truly impressive era to film viewers throughout the entire world.

Roy was to rapidly discover a veritable siege of unchanging clichés around him: walking clichés personified by travel guides, secretaries, so-called representatives of writers' clubs—who were usually political police agents—politicians, high officers, factory directors, and heads of communes. These obtrusive walking clichés absolutely infuriated him. Any attempt on his part to escape them and finally discover the truth was frustrated. In the countless conversations he had, preparing his film and his book, he sought personal statements but found only stereotyped clichés:

In the manager's waiting-room, four workers were waiting for us. I had hoped to hear other things from them than what I had been hearing elsewhere. I looked forward to an authentic sound from this direct contact with the people.... The oldest, Mr. Shin, was only forty years of age.... No snare was hidden in the question that I asked him in order to find the key I was looking for: "What has the revolution brought you?" He cleared his throat, hesitated. My question embarrassed him. He looked at his superiors, the interpreter, the mandarins in our group, and suddenly he launched into a tirade. He spoke about the proletariat oppressed by feudalism and imperialism. It was an excerpt from *Das Kapital,* or *The Manifesto of the Communist Party.* He recited his lesson very well. There was no interrupting him. I yawned. The camera stopped. The second worker, Mr. Huang, an inspector with a waxy complexion, was next in line. I tried to pinpoint him on something more down-to-earth, I asked him about his parents and his children. It was useless, he uttered only one poignant phrase: "In the old days, I never had enough to eat." Then he resumed the predecessor's obsession. "Now, thanks to Chairman Mao and the Party, we have succeeded in conquering feudalism and imperialism and we are working for peace." Madame Lio ran an assembly plant and supervised four hundred workers. She had two children. "Chairman Mao is the great savior of our country. When Peking was liberated, I felt as if they were celebrating my own liberation."... The last worker, a young woman of twenty-five, worked as a silk-winder. Her husband was employed in the same factory. Her father was a peasant. I wanted to have her say something different. "The first time that your husband rented a boat at the Summer Palace and you went rowing on the lake, did you think about Chairman Mao and the Party or did you simply feel something that swelled your heart and that is known as happiness?" The young woman was taken aback. "In the old society," she replied, "there was only a handful of profiteers. Now, the working class and the people have the right to relax."

Jules Roy is not a young man, and he has gone through a great deal. Yet oddly enough, it took him weeks to realize that he was not the chosen victim of some kind of special malice. It gradually dawned on him that the same thing happens to any traveler anywhere in China. And all of them return home with a huge mass of propaganda material and with full notebooks in which they have recorded everything that important Chinese personalities—almost always the same ones—have confided to them in special conferences. All these travelers regarded as the apogee of their voyages the encounters with prepared and rehearsed simple people, members of the masses, such as the above-quoted four workers in the Peking factory.

One need merely peruse some twenty articles, in which twenty travelers to China tell their readers what they have seen and heard, to realize that aside from minor variants the very same record has been played to all the voyagers and played back again by them.

Jules Roy, however, had come in order to find out things that were inaccessible to, or hidden from, other visitors. He was completely disappointed. The few times he happened to see people, houses, or work that didn't fit in with the clichés, every means was used to prevent him from following up on these genuine experiences. The most varied pretexts kept him away from things that would really have interested him.

And just what did he want to discover? Bad conditions? The poverty of the working people, the inconceivable backwardness of work methods, the fact that millions upon millions of Chinese still suffer daily drudgery as stand-ins for draft animals and machines? Did he merely want to see these things and derive arguments against the regime? Not at all. Jules Roy was a genuine sympathizer. He knew very well what he was going to write without embellishing or covering up the problems still in existence. He wanted to write that the Chinese people, as a result of imperialist exploitation and countless years of pillaging by the Western powers, had hit rock-bottom, and that the Communist Party had first of all restored the honor and national dignity of the Chinese, but that for a while they would be paying for this restoration with a maximum of superhuman exertion.

His opinion was totally sincere and he intended to convince his readers of it. However, the Chinese never showed him reality; they offered him a *kitsch* paradise or, more precisely, Eden painted on a facade. Everyone he spoke to always started off with the same words, summing up the execrable past and contrasting it with the blissful present. And everyone ended with a monotonous, overdone encomium of Mao Tse-tung.

> I did not arrive ... like the members of parliament who were fuddled by being housed beneath the red ceilings and golden columns of a palace, overwhelmed with princely consideration, having a huge black *zim* at their disposal, and finally being brought to uncle Mao who did his performance for them. After that, they were ripe for a combination of sinolatry and Maolatry. The great

man had shaken their hands, the hero of the Long March was interested in their health and invited them to his table. Would I have resisted myself if I had been deemed worthy to enter the inner sanctum? That was what I constantly asked myself. How can one calmly judge someone that illustrious and denounce his tics if he has offered you his friendship?

Jules Roy, the aggressive anti-Fascist of the forties, a true non-conformist and protester, lost his patience after a few weeks: despite his initial admiration of Mao Tse-tung, Roy could no longer endure the uninterrupted kowtowing to the infallible Chairman, the unrestrainable torrent of eulogies from which there was no escape.

Beloved Chairman Mao Tse-tung,
Sun that illumines our hearts!
... With you we have inaugurated the history of a new China,
With you we shall go towards the liberation of mankind.
The thousands of kilometers that you have gone are now strewn with flowers;
Your great thought, always triumphant, shines brighter and brighter,
You teach us to understand the world, to discern currents,
You teach us to reaffirm our position, to raise our desire for struggle.

Oh, beloved Chairman Mao, our great Leader,
Oh, beloved Chairman Mao, our shining paragon,
We march forward behind you,
So that some day the Red Flag may flutter everywhere.
Oh, beloved Chairman Mao, Leader of the People ...

This is not prose, this is poetry akin to that of certain contemporary authors who write editorials—usually rather

banal ones—and arrange them typographically in verse.
Jules Roy couldn't stand it, and no one can blame him.
Yet, surprisingly, he is still convinced that this frantic
Maoism is genuine and that it mirrors the thoughts and sen-
timents of all, or nearly all, Chinese.

And he is equally certain that the Chinese bureaucrats
(they were, generally, the only people he had any contact
with) genuinely adhere to the opinions they never stop repeating and are ordered to impose upon foreigners as irrevocable dogma. He writes:

> What faith? Skeptical by nature, to the point of never
> having been torn apart by religious wars, which only be-
> lievers fight, how could the Chinese people suddenly
> adopt new dogmas without keeping a secret hiding-
> place available in case of disappointment? We have to
> admit that the younger generations, raised in the cult of
> revolution, believed in their messiah, and that his com-
> plete works were their religious persuasion.

Considering the countless reports we read about China,
all this seems plausible. Since both opponents and partisans
appear to agree on this point, one might think that such conclusions are incontestable. But this is not the case.

No contemporary of Hitler's and Stalin's, particularly no
European, need take off on long voyages of exploration to realize the truth. And Germans, especially those over thirty,
know by experience. They can recall that the Nazis ran a gigantic, a demonic education and propaganda machine. Children and young people were at its mercy, not to mention the
millions of adults who, to support the Fuehrer, relinquished
the right, and even the wish, to think for themselves. And all
this could be undone and blotted out to such an extent that
as soon as everything was over quite a number of them could
maintain with a certain amount of subjective justification:
"Actually, I never really knuckled under."

But apart from this time, there are much closer experiences which no one has the right to forget. Wasn't it an established fact that the effects of Communist education were irrevocable, unchangeable, and absolutely unassailable? From right to left, the entire press throughout the world never tired of depicting an ideological and emotional commitment to Stalin as *the* universal and lasting phenomenon in the life of the Soviet nations and world communism. There were very few of us who prophesied *before* Stalin's death that afterwards some sort of reduction in totalitarian terrorism would unmask this monstrous humbug and remove it once and for all.

On June 17, 1953, a few months after Stalin died, young workers, who had spent the decisive years of their lives under the monopolitical influence of Stalinist education and propaganda, kindled the Berlin Rebellion, teaching everyone who wished to understand an unforgettable lesson. It's strange how few people pay any attention to this lesson as soon as one starts talking about China, and Mao Tse-tung, and those indefatigable eulogies. It's very strange considering the unequivocal facts of the Polish and Hungarian October of 1956 and the large-scale breaking-up process noticeable all over the Communist world.

It's even stranger, because of the extremely informative phase that China underwent in the first half of 1957: the experimental period characterized by a watchword of Mao's: "Let a hundred flowers bloom and a hundred schools of thought compete with one another!" This had been preceded by a total Maoism as frenzied and as reckless as the Maoism that Jules Roy encountered in 1964 and that awaits all visitors as the most blatant and most apparently crucial fact of life in China.

During the few months that the Chinese, and especially the intellectuals, followed the official request to speak openly and come out with whatever was on their minds and in their hearts, something horrible happened: the very same professors, philosophers, sociologists, historians, physicists, the very same writers and journalists, the very same painters, musicians, entertainers who hitherto had—so monotonously —reiterated that Mao Tse-tung was always right, that the Party never made a mistake, and that the entire nation was behind the great Mao Tse-tung and the Party, unwaveringly, completely, and unanimously—all these people and the students at universities all at once began to say out loud and to write openly that Chairman Mao Tse-tung's regime was a dictatorship against the people and not a government of, by, and for the people. All dams burst. Truth would out— irresistibly. But then the regime suddenly called off the period of flowers. Darkness came at noon, and a wintry cold broke out in the middle of July; no more mention was made of a hundred flowers, or even one. Dismissals, disciplinary measures, deportations to labor camps were once again the order of the day. The so-called period of correction began, infamous correction, in which once again black was extolled as pure white and subordination as unanimity and blissful harmony.

Naturally, Jules Roy knows all this. He had read about it before his trip, and his great disappointment was all the more reason for taking it into consideration. Yet he almost totally ignores it, because like so many pro- and non-Communist reporters he continues to believe that the cliché-automatons who came along on his tour and constantly tried to make him listen to reason never said anything they didn't actually think or feel.

Jules Roy, while writing this, still believes that this is the true will of the people:

No one has the right to receive even his own mother in his home without notifying the island head. This is one of the rules to which all submit to safeguard the State. Nor would anyone ever dream of protesting because a neighbor, suspected of being lukewarm, is sent off to fan his ardor in a popular commune.

We once read similar things about the Russian people's unquestionable approval of Stalin's measures or the Hungarian people's enthusiasm for Rakosi's police force. So we don't have to go to China to realize that Jules Roy, like most reporters, is making a mistake. One reason for this is, as we have said, his taking the eulogies of Mao at face value; furthermore, he was so filled with admiration of this Chinese demigod that he wanted to transmute Mao's rise to power and his legendary Long March into a cinematic sensation. Like numerous other leftist intellectuals who may no longer be Stalinists but will not make do with Castroism, Jules Roy still believes that Mao has created an original theory of revolution.

This is as invalid as a belief in Mao Tse-tung's originality as a general, as the creator of strategy for guerrillas and partisan warfare. Even the superficial connoisseur of Marxism knows that Marx foresaw the possibility of a revolutionary role for the Russian peasant such as proletarian Messianism never prognosticated. Lenin and his disciples repeatedly adverted to this possibility and quoted certain passages from Marx, especially from the letters, which formulated this so-called Mao Tse-tung Theory.

Before leaving China, Jules Roy was received by Vice-Chairman Marshal Chen Yi, who usually grants a lengthy audience to nearly all intellectual pilgrims from the West, especially the French-speaking ones, at the end of their pilgrimage, and offers them long speeches. Chen Yi began his conversation with the following words:

"Since you're a writer, let me put you on guard. Anatole

France said that literary criticism is an adventure of the mind. Your criticism, if its nature is political, could easily expose you to an even greater danger. The book you intend to write will testify to the success or failure of your venture. Stalin said that the writer is the engineer of the soul. If your book is malicious, it can only occasion regrettable results. I recall that Chairman Mao Tse-tung once told an old Chinese philosopher that writing could both save or destroy lives. The pen is thus more fearful than the sword."

These banalities, recited momentously and homogenized with worn-out quotations, might have made some impression on the writer before he set out for China, and the veiled threats might even have had some influence on him. But now it was too late:

". . . it is true, and I won't deny it, that I saw almost nothing with the eyes of faith; and it is true that my former faith was gone. I only know I came to China full of love and admiration and that I left bitter and terrorized. . . . The dream that spurred me will continue for a long time to spur the tourist-groups traveling at a reduced rate, the black African students in a quest of brotherhood and the M.P.'s of capitalist countries eager to discover the secrets of success."

What successes? Elsewhere Roy says that Marxism-Leninism-Maoism has succeeded in totally wiping out the cultural traditions of China, including the worship of ancestors, and transforming an anti-militaristic people into a nation of soldiers. But the deeply disappointed writer is as mistaken as he was when blinded by enthusiasm.

One of the most characteristic delusions of many of our contemporaries is their mistaking the momentary effects of totalitarian power for a magical metamorphosis brought about by an ideology. We needn't even leave our homes to discover that wherever dictatorial power is totalitarian, it degrades the people at its mercy to the point of seemingly fanatical self-effacement. They may be degraded, however, but basically they remain undefeated and their innermost being remains unchanged.

The pilgrim to Utopia grasps this only after the sorrowful realization that Utopia is not a land, but a part of ourselves, that it is one of our inner landscapes.

January 1966

The False Alternative

~~~~~~

A FTER the passage of so many years we still have not forgotten the course of events that began early one morning
in July 1936 in a mood of daring optimism only to reach a
dismal end two years and 254 days later. Since then, it has
been painful to think of Spain and impossible not to think
of the soldiers who, in the darkness of unmerited defeat,
were forced to disown their beliefs, driven as these men were
by the fear of dying for nothing and disgusted by the instinct
to survive no matter what.

The bitter taste of defeat has never left us, the lost Republic has never stopped haunting us like useless regret.
Even when we heard the cries for help during the Warsaw
uprising, or, nine years later, the appeal uttered by the
workers of East Berlin, or when, on November 4, 1956, the
alarming cry of the Hungarian Revolution plunged us into
despair—every single appeal brought back the mournful
voice of Spain: an echo calling the voices to which it replied.

There were so many of us who have never forgotten that
the Western world, by its despicable refusal to act at the beginning of the Spanish Civil War, is guilty of a shame that it
still hasn't blotted out.

The Republic had been invaded by an army of mercenaries and colonial troops whose commanding officers were no longer able to defeat anyone but their own unarmed people. To disgrace the young Republic, the invaders plunged her into gory chaos. They were determined to annihilate the new democracy before it could abolish ancient privileges, return the soil to the peasants and the land to the nation, or attach Spain to modern Europe.

The Republic needed the immediate help of the democratic countries, especially France and England. Yet these two powers opted for a policy of timorous indifference, to which they applied the label of Nonintervention.

The high season of cowardice that had begun in 1933 was now reaching its climax. Nineteen-forty merely brought a period of interruption; for in May 1945 at the very latest, the season of cowardice recommenced in all free countries.

The first result of Nonintervention was to provide the Francoist counterrevolution with the time needed by Hitler and Mussolini to provide unlimited military aid. A further issue of the French and English policy was its making of Stalin the sole patron of the mortally threatened Spanish democracy. And thus it only took a year to achieve a totalitarian polarization in Spain.

From that point on, Spain served the two competing systems of totalitarian dictatorship as a test battlefield. The deadliest fraud of our century perverted the meaning and purpose of the revolution. The Spanish people still fought against the Tercio, the Falangists, and the Fascist divisions, but the goals for which the defenders of the Republic risked their lives became unattainably remote.

Although the Stalinists were paid solid gold for the armaments they supplied to the Republic they secretly insisted on having access to all command posts of any importance. After the NKVD had murdered the great proletarian leader Andrés Nin, it staged a Moscow-type trial in Barcelona, in

October 1937, against Julian Gorkin, Andrade, Arquer, Bonet, and the other leaders of the POUM, the anti-Stalinist workers' party. The ultimate aim was to force upon both the international Left and the Spanish Republicans a single alternative: either unconditional subordination to Stalin and his men or unconditional surrender to Franco and his allies.

And the Fascists, for their part, used the very same fraud of a false alternative. Nor has anyone forgotten that the Church never failed to aggravate this baleful polarization. Before the Spanish people could even lay down their arms they realized that they were being menaced on two sides: by the Spain of the past, which was cruelly destroying the present and their hopes—and by their own friends. By those friends who had clapped the new democracy into the vise of a totalitarian alternative and were giving it the final turn of the screw, and by the other friends who, like spectators at a bullfight, were waiting suspensefully for the "moment of truth" in which the protagonists are finally allowed to die after a protracted agony.

For fifty years now, the totalitarian pseudoalternative of the most menacing extortion of our time has been offering its doubly false arguments: the murder of Rosa Luxemburg and Karl Liebknecht, of Kurt Eisner, Gustav Landauer, and so many other Socialists and Communists in Germany; the murder of Matteoti; the Fascist Reign of Terror in Italy; the infamous crimes of the semi-Fascist regimes in the Balkans and the Latin-American countries; and finally the permanent atrocities of Nazism. All the dictators and their myrmidons, their diplomats and their tractable intellectuals rationalized the fury of dictatorship by claiming: "Anyone opposing us helps the Communists and aids them in taking over. Never forget for even a single moment that you've got to choose between them and us! So make your choice!"

At the same time, Stalin's propagandists announced everywhere: "Whoever goes so far as to criticize forcible collectivization or the suppression of the opposition or the administrative deportation to Siberia, whoever goes so far as to carp at the Moscow Trials, is for Mussolini and against the exiles of the Lipari Islands, is for Hitler and against his victims in Dachau, Oranienburg, and Buchenwald, is for Franco and against the murdered population of Guernica. There is no other choice than between them and us."

The great extortionists are gone; no day elapses without their former henchmen and bootlickers frantically disavowing them. The posthumous fate of these supermen reveals more clearly than any crime of theirs how grotesquely similar they were to one another: it was their ambition alone that transformed them into rivals, and their rivalry that made them implacable enemies.

The old general who, eighteen years after the infamous end of the *Führer* and the *Duce,* still has people call him *El Caudillo,* executed the leading Communist official Julian Grimau in circumstances that were loathsome in every way. This Spanish émigré had been sent from abroad by the Communist Party to organize an illegal Communist movement at home. He attempted to do so, and thus, according to the law, he committed a crime. Yet this was not the reason why Grimau was brought before a military tribunal: he was tried allegedly for a crime not provided for in the books; he was declared guilty of the "permanent crime of military rebellion." This term is provokingly meaningless because it was applicable—if at all—not to the specific case of Grimau, but rather to one single person: Franco. The defenseless prisoner was ruthlessly tortured, sentenced to death in a mock trial, and then killed hastily and insidiously.

This *Caudillo* appears to believe that extortion is as use-

ful today as in the days of Hitler and Stalin. He thinks that
everything is speedily passing into oblivion—especially any
act of injustice that remains irreparable. For example, the
murder of Imre Nagy and his men, whom Kadar executed
immediately after a mock trial. The Attorney General explained: "A *fait accompli* has a tranquilizing effect on the
people."

Franco's ministers, all of whom voted for the execution of
Julian Grimau, had assuredly not forgotten this encouraging
aphorism. But mainly they counted on the effectiveness of
the anti-Communist ploy. They assumed they could reckon
with at least the tacit approval of the anti-Stalinists, since the
man being executed was actually one of the heads of the Stalinist NKVD in Barcelona.

And no doubt, had Grimau come to power, he would always have remained obedient to the changing orders from
Moscow and behaved no differently from a Rakosi, a Gerö, a
Gottwald—or a Kadar. Yet this doesn't alter the facts, nor
does it lessen our indignation at what the Spanish dictatorship did to this man; it doesn't modify our duty to protest in
unequivocal terms against a shameless mockery of justice.
For so many years now, we have been resolutely challenging
the false alternative of Hitler and Stalin, or Franco and
Kadar.

"The fury of fools fills the world with its roaring." This
sad refrain from *Les Grands Cimetières sous la Lune* is not
forgotten. Georges Bernanos wrote this indispensable book
after realizing how wrong the alternative was that others had
attempted to confront him with in the name of the Church
and the "holiest goods."

Like the murderers of Imre Nagy, *El Caudillo* is speculat-
ing on the pseudodialectic of totalitarian logic which trans-
mogrifies those who fall prey to it into furious blockheads
raging on command.

"You can see that there is only one opposition in Spain—the Communist movement led by the same men who committed dreadful crimes during the Civil War. Any fair dealings with this opposition will merely promote the cause of communism and eventually lead to a new Civil War." Such is the reasoning used by the Francoists to secure the angry approval of political blockheads and at the same time to tranquilize the people with a *fait accompli*.

Everywhere in the world the Communists are proclaiming: "The only real opposition in Spain is the Communist movement. And it is so effective and dangerous that Franco, panic-stricken and at his wits' end, had to get rid of Grimau as quickly as possible. Anyone who is not with us helps Franco; and anyone who is against his dictatorship has got to join us and refuse to criticize us."

The truth of the matter is that the entire Spanish people abominates the Civil War and its violence as much as it despises all dictatorships. The Spanish people's wounds have barely healed; and for this reason, too, they desire more than anything the ultimate reconciliation of all Spaniards within a democratic state that guarantees all human rights to each and every citizen.

The truth of the matter is that the Spanish wish to join the free nations. Europe, which did nothing twenty-five years ago to save the young democracy, now has the obligation to vouchsafe a chosen place to a free Spain that is developing despite everything. The Western world will have many possibilities of blotting out a terrible sin. Yet no one can help Spain by tacitly tolerating a murder, the murder of a man who survived the Civil War; we cannot tolerate his murder no matter what his past may be.

1963

The Mihajlov Case

~~~~~~

THE UNRESOLVED PAST
OF COMMUNISM

THE man who has outgrown his childhood still belongs
to the past in many ways. Everything we have experienced, done, and suffered has not flowed away like water in a
river; consciously or unconsciously, it has been stored. We
harbor the past we have lived through like time congealed,
and we are ourselves both a present in development and a
changing past.

"One cannot rule without becoming culpable," proclaimed the French revolutionary Saint-Just 170 years ago.
Nor can one live without being responsible and thereby—to
a greater or lesser degree—culpable. Nobody dies innocent,
for no one has lived innocent.

The phrase *the unresolved past*, which has emerged and
become fashionable in Germany, has always been meaningful and valid for the individual, psychologically and ethi-
cally. Yet it is no coincidence that modern-day psychology,
especially psychoanalysis, stresses that a human being can
and must develop illness as a result of not coming to terms
with past events and experiences. The more he represses
them, the less he has managed to cope with them. And the
less he copes with them, the greater his compulsion to repress them.

This is particularly true of the individual into whose life

the totalitarian despotism of our era has forced a new dimension. To make this clear, it will be useful at least to outline a comparison between contemporary dictatorships and the despotic reigns of the past. The absolute ruler and his supporting classes attributed their position to the grace of God; they never required ideological pretexts and never claimed the approval—much less the enthusiasm—of the people. The old tyrannies were completely negative: they forbade certain actions, utterances, and public expressions of opinion insofar as these could cast doubt upon the privileges and the prestige of the rulers; everything else they left to the priests or even the discretion of the subjects. In contrast, totalitarian despotism is, so to speak, positive: it does not wait to forbid; it forces the 100 per cent (or at least 98 per cent) enthusiastic approval of the people. It never claims to exist by the grace of God, but simply to embody the entire nation and, moreover, to be national-socialist or communistic—the people's dream come true. Such a dictatorship is consequently never content with merely wiping out all opposition: it forces; it extorts jubilation, eternal praise.

The fiction of the absolute acceptance of the totalitarian state obliges it to be re-elected daily, systematically organizing the farce of elections without opposing candidates, mass demonstrations and congresses, and popular eruptions of fury against adversaries. Modern despotism is no longer content to deprive the opposition of power. It uses radical means to enforce silence, self-disavowal, or death. Mussolini, Hitler, and Stalin secured their daily ration of false identity, with which the people assure the dictator that he is the sole source of all truth and wisdom, a situation in which any opposition, even the slightest dissent, is as inconceivable as denial of the light of day at high noon. Differing opinion is consequently considered not so much the expression of a divergent attitude as deception, a mask behind which the enemy is seeking concealment. The totalitarian regime forces its subjects into a terrible complicity. Saint-Just's observation has to be extended in the twentieth century to read: "It is terribly difficult to be a subject in a dictatorship without becoming an accomplice."

Thus for some fifty years the notion of an unresolved past has been reaching beyond the individual psyche. If we fail to comprehend this, we will understand little about contemporary man. And we will understand little or nothing about his psyche if we believe we can be rid of the past simply by acting as if nothing had happened or as if whatever did happen has been filed away and forgotten. The malefactor may have forgotten his crime (although, psychologically, he will never do so completely), but as long as there exists a single survivor, no amount of forgetting will remove anything. And, as total as a crime may be, there is always at least one survivor in whose memory it is lodged.

Another element in this context merits the attention of the psychologist as well as that of the sociologist and the historian: once the accomplices' identification of dictator and nation is invalid—when the terror is over and the right to seek and speak the truth has been restored—the guilt-laden people feel retrospectively humiliated. There is a perfectly understandable tendency in the individual and the group to avoid any memory of humiliation.

This statement also applies to the unresolved past of communism, for example in the case of Mihajlo Mihajlov, a teacher of literature in Yugoslavia. This case is significant insofar as the persecution he left himself open to is seen as an episode in the struggle against the past and for its resolution. The significance holds not only for Party members, who served Stalinism without the slightest qualms, but also for the legion of people who, although not members of the Party, helped spread the murderous legend of Stalin and insulted, denigrated, and persecuted his opponents. Far beyond the borders of the countries in which the totalitarian Satans ruled, those non-Party members incessantly spread the totalitarian confusion without which endless moral and intellectual destruction would not have been possible.

The typical experience of our era thus became that of countless contemporaries: the perversion of word and meaning, of essence and deed. It was perversion that always began the same way: the demagogues and dictators branded loyalty treason and lauded the betrayal of ideas and human beings as exemplary virtues; they labeled the victims persecutors, regarded the unscrupulous persecutors of the innocent as saviors of justice, and praised the patent propaganda liars as fanatics of truth. Therefore, when we speak of the unresolved past of Nazism or Stalinism, we tend to refer to the problem of complicity in regard to incredible actions and an incomprehensible intellectual degeneracy.

Mihajlo Mihajlov tried to grapple with this problem in *Delo,* a Belgrade periodical, which ran the first two parts of his travelogue "Moscow, Summer 1964." The author, who taught Russian literature at the University of Zadar, had visited the Soviet Union several times, the last time as a so-called cultural exchange guest.

The third section of this report of several hundred pages never appeared in print; *Delo* was severely rebuked for bringing out the first two parts, publicly attacked, and threatened with suppression.

What was wrong? Had any of the readers protested? Not at all! In reality, "Moscow, Summer 1964" had been regarded by readers concerned with literary matters as a revealing document, of interest even to those who did not agree with its conclusions and judgments on books and writers.

The interference had another source: Marshal Tito.

Shortly after the second part appeared, Tito received a dele-
gation of Yugoslavia's leading district attorneys. In his speech
to them (published on March 4), he reproached his guests
for frequently failing to act against political crimes and try
the felons:

Have you seen what happened with an article in *Delo?*
The district attorney should have forbidden the publication and made the matter public. The author of the
article should have been severely criticized, an inquiry
should have been announced, an inquiry into a reac-
tionary who slandered a great event: the October Revolution. We are a socialist country. We cannot remain indifferent. . . . It is really odd that such things can
happen here despite the existence of workers' councils
in the press and in printer's plants.

Tito had a great deal more on his mind, but he finally
came back to the article in question:

In our socialist country we cannot allow anyone to do
what has been done here: to justify the Nazi concentration camps in which millions of old people and children
were cremated alive. No Marxist, no decent person
could ever tolerate our lack of action in such cases.

Tito went on to speak in great detail about the relationship between the district attorney's office and the political
organization and finally expressed his views on the situation
of the press. He recalled *Perspectives,* a Slovenian periodical
that had already been suppressed:

This is not simply a question of Slovenian Perspectives,
for similar instances can be found in Zagreb, Belgrade,
Novisad, and Sarajevo—everywhere. My impression is
that we are dealing with something comparable to *Djilasism.* . . . The propagation of such ideas through the
press is *extremely dangerous.*

Dangerous indeed. We shall see how and why. But first I would like to take issue with one of Tito's statements. There is nothing whatsoever in Mihajlov's "Moscow, Summer 1964" justifying Hitler's death camps.

For various reasons, I am one of those certainly not infrequent contemporaries for whom no day passes without a reminder of the Nazi crimes. It is thus all the more my duty to explain that totalitarian rulers always indulge in an unbearable, impudent, and stupid blackmail: they attempt to divert attention from their own crimes by claiming that any disclosure thereof merely glosses over the crimes of the opposition. This blackmail creates a false alternative; cholera does not make the Plague more pleasant. Hitler's crimes do not justify Stalinism. Stalin's atrocities in no way justify the mass murders of the Nazis. If we multiply one injustice by another, the product is not justice but multiple injustice.

Let us look at Mihajlov's text itself, especially a statement that gets to the heart of our problem:

> Thus, there exists in the USSR an ambivalent relationship to both Stalinism and to those who fight against it. On the one hand, Stalinism is condemned as working against the people and declared criminal. Yet anti-Stalinism is also condemned. An abnormal situation of this kind has to be cleared up sooner or later, and since the anti-Stalinists are very much on the offensive today, this problem, as far as we can judge, will soon be on the agenda.

Sooner than we think. It is already being discussed. Tito calls it *Djilasism* and wants his judges to get rid of it behind prison walls. But just what is Djilasism? Simply the belated but not overly tardy courage and decency of a Communist leader or official willing to admit his responsibility as at least a mental accomplice of the crimes of the Stalinist regime, thus helping truth to out. This means, among other things, putting an end to all falsification of history and exposing the fraud of the so-called rehabilitations. It is downright insulting of the murderers and their accomplices to claim they can rehabilitate innocent victims when they themselves—who are the cause of huge, endless suffering—should be made responsible for their deeds.

Just how did Mihajlov's account anger Tito and the diplomats? Not by the reiteration of the author's more or less interesting conversations with a large number of younger and a few older writers. These talks are interesting and sometimes both biographically, sociologically, and literarily informative—but they contain quite a bit of material that has been articulated and printed elsewhere. A comment like that of old Leonid Leonov that the only really important problem in the Soviet Union is to ferret out and definitively remove the causes of Stalinism will, however, sound dangerous to a number of ears. All the more so because he adds that the authorities are still doing everything they can to inhibit liberalization. But Leonov's most dreadful observation was that "People will be writing about Soviet concentration camps for a long time, for the next eighty years."

Mihajlov goes on to report that this highly respected writer has been rewriting his own books for quite a while, because originally he had to write them in such a way as not to fall under the suspicion of the regime. Only now can he "come to himself," as it were. Even the reader who is no writer and has no special relationship to literature can easily imagine what it must mean to a creative person constantly to censor, distort, and maim his own works beyond recognition. Leonid Leonov has spent the last few years at his desk cleaning up his life's work.

It is obvious that Mihajlov's unpopularity was particularly a result of the fact that he recalled the Soviet concentration camps and noted that they were actually built more than ten years before the Nazi camps: "Symptomatically, the Soviet press refers less and less to Fascism and the Nazi camps and avoids any comparison to and with the Soviet camps. This is understandable. The first 'death camps' were built by the Soviets, not the Germans. In 1921, near Archangelsk, the first 'death-camp,' Holmogor, began operating. Its sole purpose was the physical annihilation of the prisoners. It functioned successfully for years, swallowing up former comrades—the members of non-Bolshevist revolutionary parties (Social Revolutionaries, Mensheviks, *et al.*)." Elsewhere Mihajlov writes:

> A doctoral candidate at the University of Moscow told me: "They've only rehabilitated their own people. But what about the thousands of decent people who aren't members of the Party?" Many Soviet citizens with whom I came into contact gave me sarcastic accounts about the ways and means of rehabilitation. The family receives a standard certificate with the first and last name of the victim and the official confirmation of rehabilitation—that's all. Nobody knows where, when, or how the "rehabilitated" man died. And there's no way of finding out. Since there are few Soviet families without at least one "rehabilitated" member, there is quite a general dissatisfaction about this semi-liquidation of Stalinism. However, most people are deeply convinced that the fight against Stalinism has only just begun, and most of us are optimistic about the outcome.

Mihajlov goes into great detail about the immense importance that the Soviet concentration camps used to have in the personal lives of Soviet citizens, and he constantly points out how vivid this recent past remains not only in the memory of the victims but also in the minds of their families and friends. Everywhere, especially in the field of literature, he found this a pervasive and permanent theme. He correctly quotes Khrushchev, who publicly declared in 1963 that periodicals and publishing houses had already received about ten thousand novels, stories, and memoirs centering around the theme of the camps. Mihajlov feels that this number is not surprisingly high if we recall that (according to very conservative estimates) between eight and twelve million people were deported to those camps.

The whole world knows Alexander Solzhenitsin's extremely moving novel *A Day in the Life of Ivan Denisovich.* But not all readers are aware that this book enraged the reactionaries among the Russian literary functionaries, who attacked the author and his work even more ferociously than they had attacked Dudintsev and his novel *Man Does Not Live by Bread Alone.* This time, however, there were many more writers and journalists courageous enough to defend the assaulted book.

It is to Mihajlov's credit that he indicated numerous other books even the titles of which are nearly unknown in the Western world that also depict totalitarian reality so truthfully one can only read them with great anguish. Mihajlov quotes, among other writings, the memoirs of General Gorbatov, who was imprisoned in Soviet penitentiaries and camps from 1938 to 1941:

"The guards, with the warden in the lead, got along excellently with the criminals, supporting their violent inclinations and using them to deride the 'enemies of the people.' ... The hard labor was regularly assigned to the 'enemies of the people,' the easier work to the 'friends,' i.e., the criminals." One might think that this came from one of the many accounts of German concentration camps.

Elsewhere in his account, Gorbatov recalls the cruel practice of collective family imprisonment. The women's camps contained "... our mothers, wives, sisters, daughters usually condemned as members of families. . . . If we hadn't broken any law, we were at least accused of something, but these poor unfortunates were nothing but the victims of a cruel and blatant autocracy."

None of this is really new to Western readers. At times one almost feels as if the naïve but certainly honest general, a renowned war hero, had simply copied from a dozen of those books that have come out here since 1945 only to be branded *in toto* by the Communists and their sympathizers as a horrible slander and completely ignored by the critics.

General Gorbatov joins the innumerable innocents who were arrested without basis, tortured physically and mentally into confessing and bearing the blame for a dreadful crime that usually had not been committed and was entirely the product of the NKVD's imagination. Gorbatov doesn't reveal anything new, yet his persistence in following the Khrushchev line by indicating only Stalin and the personality cult instead of a whole regime is intolerable. Even so, Gorbatov has a few virtually innocuous indications of drawing closer to the real problem; he writes: "During an interrogation I accidentally discovered the name of one of the interrogating monsters: Stolbunsky. I don't know his present whereabouts."

The fact that it wasn't just a personality cult means that Stolbunsky and his sort are still alive, comfortably in office, and have been promoted frequently on the basis of seniority. Nothing happened to them; the Khrushchevs, the Kosygins, and the Brezhnevs are their protectors, because they have to shield themselves and their own past.

Who then is coming to grips with the past, which still remains a frightening present and, as Leonid Leonov predicts, will disturb minds until the middle of the next century?

In his intelligent, frequently naïve, but thoroughly sincere account, Mihajlov mentions a Soviet phenomenon of the time, one we have been totally unaware of up till now: the folklore of the camps. He asserts that songs originating in the camps and probably composed by the prisoners have been spreading about for a number of years and enjoying an unusual popularity everywhere. The authorities have not yet allowed these songs to be recorded, but since many Russians can do tapings of these songs, they can be heard all over. One of them, which comes from the infamous camp of Magadam on the peninsula of Kola, begins:

> Damn you, Kola,
> I'll lose my mind,
> For I'll never go home from here.
> I know that nobody's waiting for me,
> Nobody's reading my letters.
> And nobody will come
> To welcome me.
> But if anyone were to come
> He wouldn't recognize me.

The final stanza of another song goes:

> If, lined up, you say a single word
> They'll pull you out with tongs
> And the next day the order will come
> To throw you into the shed.

One is reminded of the songs the Tsarist prisoners sang en route to Siberia. Yet in those days the prisoners were greeted everywhere by the active sympathy the Russian people are capable of and that they were not forbidden to show. One need merely check in Dostoevski's *House of the Dead*.

At the end of the third part of his report (published in the Free World but not in Yugoslavia), Mihajlov sketches out a kind of psychology of *homo sovieticus*—his name for the Soviet citizen who has become a perfect product of Communist upbringing and the regime, the model of an obedient subject, demonstrating his pious kowtowing to the authorities in feeling, thought, and deed, prepared to do anything they require of him.

Mihajlov quotes from Dostoevski's famous political novel, *The Possessed,* the lines in which the great writer characterizes Erkel, a proto-*homo sovieticus* born a hundred years too early: "Carrying out orders has always been a need of petty, ungifted natures who are always prepared to knuckle under to someone else's will in order to serve the universal and great cause. . . . Of all of Shatoff's murderers, Erkel was the most unfeeling—he didn't even feel any personal hatred for his victims."

> *Homo sovieticus* seems, to an outside observer [Mihajlov writes], above all immature. He is so naïve that he is capable of believing his own lies; he deliberately closes his eyes to anything that might unmask his lifelong lie. Consciously or unconsciously, he invokes the highest end to excuse even the worst baseness. This is part of the psychology of the average *homo sovieticus.* . . . He considers it unthinkable, nay, absurd and impossible that anyone might publicly express a personal opinion except in total concord with the party line and the official policies. . . . The psychology of *homo sovieticus* contains a powerful streak of mental plebeianism and lacks all intellectual nobility. . . . The relationship to the leader is that of a servant in love with his boss—and this is manifest in almost all realms of life.

Every German was well acquainted with this *homo sovieticus,* not in the Soviet Union but in the Third Reich, in his own city, his own street, perhaps in his own house or even his own family. *Homo sovieticus,* prevalent in every country, is both the creator and the creature of the totalitarian regime—fascist or Stalinist.

The day Tito's attack was published, Mihajlov was arrested and indicted for jeopardizing good relations between Yugoslavia and Russia. The same Tito who accused Mihajlov of using the Soviet camps to vindicate the Nazis and disparage the October Revolution had made a speech on July 28, 1951, asserting that "an unprecedented crime of genocide was being committed" in the Soviet Union, that "whole nations were being annihilated before the very eyes of the entire world." His speech, a retort to Soviet attacks against Titoism, had ended with a rhetorical question: "Who then is a criminal, who is committing genocide, who is exterminating nations and practicing mass murder?"

Some sixteen months later, at the second Party Congress of Yugoslav Communists, Tito had declared: "Millions of Soviet citizens are languishing in forced labor in death camps, millions of members of non-Russian peoples in the Soviet Union have been wiped out—and in such a cruel fashion that even Hitler could be envious."

These were Tito's words on November 3, 1952, in Zagreb. Was he lying? Or was he telling a truth that he now condemns as a slanderous lie because it does not serve his present purpose? Whatever the reason, we can see that in 1951 the truth about Stalinism and its crimes could be circulated freely in Yugoslavia. Well, not completely freely, for the Stalinist past of Tito and his comrades was not to be delved into. And so a number of books, including Weissberg-Cybulski's *Witches' Sabbath* and Margarete Buber-Neumann's *A Prisoner of Stalin and Hitler,* were translated into Serbian, Croatian, and Slovenian and published in huge editions.

On March 4, 1964, Mihajlov was indicted in accordance with Paragraph 175, section I, article 125 of the newspaper law and held in custody for thirty-seven days. A short time earlier, Belgrade's weekly *Nin* had run an article in the characteristic style of Stalinist vilification! Against Mihajlov, his parents, his activities, his writings, and his ideas. Then something happened that probably neither the editor of the paper nor Tito and the officious justice department had foreseen. The victim under attack defended himself: he sent a courageous—better, aggressive—retort addressed to the editor, and since he assumed that neither he nor any of the 270 editors receiving copies of his rejoinder would print it, he also wrote a letter to Western newspapers, including a copy for the Belgrade correspondent of *The New York Times*. Furthermore, he sent the complete manuscript of "Moscow, Summer 1964," including the third part of his reportage, to Giovanni Volte, a publisher in Rome. As if this were not enough, Mihajlov wrote to Tito himself, complaining about the vitriolic campaign the Marshal's speech had unleashed against him.

His opponents soon realized that there were a goodly number of us throughout the world who regarded the case of this young Yugoslav as a barometer of freedom in Yugoslavia and of Titoist servility toward the Soviet Union. This was not without consequence for Yugoslavia, for at that very moment the international PEN club was about to hold its annual congress in Bled, a spa in Slovenia.

Literary messengers from Belgrade arrived in Paris, London, and other Western centers to tell us confidentially:

1. Mihajlov, whose parents are from Russia, had an uncle in Moscow who belonged to the NKVD. It was on his behalf and as a favor to him that Mihajlov visited all those Russian writers and, without their realizing it, taped what they said. He then handed all those tapes over to his uncle in the NKVD.

2. His entire account was untrue. Soviet writers are completely free and not subject to even the slightest pressure; they have nothing to fear.

3. By publishing his report, Mihajlov had compromised and denounced all the writers he had seen, jeopardizing them and exposing them to prosecution and many other difficulties.

So much for the accommodating messengers. There is no need here to comment on or disprove this incoherent conglomeration of clumsy slander and malevolent accusation. In any event, no one paid the least attention to the messages. The protest action for Mihajlov, effectively sparked by English intellectuals, evoked a powerful echo almost everywhere; PEN had obviously provided effective help in a more diplomatic way. The decisive thing, however, was the victim's courage. His trial took place on April 29 and 30 in the lawcourt of Zadar. The court was filled with students and professors whose sympathy with the young teacher was clear to all.

One important fact—to the credit of the present regime in Yugoslavia—must be mentioned. This was not a Stalinist trial; the defendant was not transformed into his own deadly enemy; he was not forced to play the part of an informer and district attorney against himself. Nevertheless, Mihajlov, through his manly bravery, performed a great service for himself and all Yugoslav intellectuals as well as for the cause of freedom. He could just as easily have retreated and maneuvered to get into the good graces of the judges. But he would do nothing of the sort. He simply asserted over and over again that he had written the truth, stating that historical truths could not be revised on command.

When asked why he had likened the Soviet camps to the Nazi ones, Mihajlov replied: "That was no accident. I believe that Stalinism is no better than Fascism, and that's why I made that comparison. . . . Totalitarianism is the same everywhere, no matter what banner it may wave, no matter what social order it may strive to realize."

Asked why he had applied the word *genocide,* he simply
answered: "This word describes the facts that I have reported."

The Polish-Croatian lawyer Dr. Ivo Glowacky, a survivor
of the Austrian Empire, defended Mihajlov intelligently,
without provoking the court or the regime but also without
flattering them in the least. He decisively asked that Mihajlov be acquitted.

The defendant declared in a concluding statement: "I
shall continue to write as I have been writing. If the court
sentences me, it will also be condemning historiography, for
then the historian will be forced to proceed along guidelines
that dictate to him what he may assert to be historical truth
and what not."

Before completing his final statement, Mihajlov posed a
momentous question: "Which of Stalin's SS-Kommandants
and concentration-camp myrmidons have ever been put on
trial? Who, when, and where?"

And he terminated his courageous counterattack by quoting a statement Bertrand Russell had made in 1951: "Both
Communists and Nazis have tragically proven that a major
portion of mankind feels the urge to torture others and that
these people need merely the opportunity of revealing this
instinct in its naked horror."

Mihajlov received a sentence of nine months' imprisonment, which he immediately appealed—and he won, for the
higher court reversed the judgment, acquitting him of having broken the law as set down in Paragraph 175 of the Yugoslav criminal code. The court of appeal thus confirmed the
accusations that Tito had hurled against the Communist regime of the Soviet Union in 1951–1952 and that Mihajlov's
travelogue had reiterated some thirteen years later.

Who overcomes the past, I asked. Let us recall the Biblical tale of the Israelites, released from Egyptian bondage and

wandering on and on through the desert. People may need such long wanderings to deliver themselves from a past of enslavement. Survival isn't enough; one must "overdie" the past.

This is the problem for the younger generation—both in Russia and in Germany, and anywhere a dictatorship has reigned long enough to destroy a large number of people, not just physically but morally as well. We are all too familiar with the strange situation of a father unable to answer when his sons and daughters ask the apparently simple question: "How could you allow all those terrible things to happen? How could you tolerate it? How could you go along with it, how could you speak out against the innocent victims and brazenly flatter the leaders?"

What is now going on in the Soviet Union and what Mihajlov describes in his "Moscow, Summer 1964" is to a great extent the barely perceptible, yet more and more general moral and intellectual rebellion of a new generation.

Let us be equitable: it *is* true, of course, that those of us who have never been put to the test can easily criticize. We can act as if we had proved ourselves, since we have been spared the opportunity of copping-out or degenerating.

Accordingly, one could naturally assert that the sons have a very easy time of it. But this does not matter. Mihajlov speaks of a growing number of young poets, writers, philosophers, and artists who simply reject their legacy. They refuse to participate in either the guilt of their fathers or the entire tissue of lies of a dogmatized and idolized ideology. This younger generation is resolved to speak out openly, precisely because the guilt-laden adults have forgotten the meaning of candor and always took it for granted that they must first inquire as to what may and what may not be spoken.

The younger generation is interested in the past, in the Great Purge of the thirties, the Siberian camps. This is astonishing when one thinks of today's German youth. How shall we explain this contradiction? The first reason of course is that the Russian camps have only been releasing their prisoners during the last ten years. A further reason, superficial but cogent, is the fact that there is hardly a family in the Soviet Union that hasn't had at least one member in a camp. The third reason, more profound, is that Russian youth is seeking a new and independent path. Today's young people in Russia are amazingly reminiscent of the younger generations there that have succeeded one another since the Decembrist Rebellion in 1825. They recall the heroes in Turgenev, especially in *Fathers and Sons,* the heroes of Dostoevski, whose novels are being devoured by a whole new audience in Russia, and the heroes in Leonid Andreyev, Gorki, and their contemporaries.

These young people are seeking their path. Today they are, or are about to become, essentially nihilistic. No wonder, for they live between the ruins of demolished temples. They move among idols in which no one believes. Russia, a home for ideologies since the Napoleonic wars, is now ideologically neutralized despite official ideologism. The young people Mihajlov encountered, although automatically reiterating some cliché or other of Soviet state dogma, actually had no conception of any future or any social order they considered a necessary and promising object of struggle.

It may be that one can only rid oneself of the burden of a criminal past completely if he regards that past in the light of a new vision. Perhaps.

The question at the nexus of a "strategy of freedom" would be "How does one really become free?" This is a psychological question that confronts every human being at some point in his life. How does one regain lost freedom without bloody fighting, without civil war, and without the risk of an unleashed violence once again setting up a new regime of bondage in the name of freedom?

This problem is on the agenda, not only in Russia, China, and the satellite countries, but also (in a different form and to a lesser degree) in Spain, Portugal, Cuba, and other nations in Latin America, Asia, and Africa. After two terrible world wars, it is beyond all doubt a grave matter influencing every decision. The freedom fighters fear the consequences of violence and thus are loath to bring about ardently yearned-for changes by means of civil war. The main battle is consequently being fought in a secondary theater of war, so to speak: in the realm of ideas—within certain intellectual circles, such as at Spanish universities. The cardinal issues there are naturally not questions of statutes in student organizations but the ultimate resolution and liquidation of a terrible past and the rebirth of a new free Spain.

The aims and issues are the same in all dictatorships. But the despots are not deceiving themselves when, as if frightened by a nightmare, they temporarily end a period of tolerance of what they consider terrible events, the spreading desire for free expression.

"This sort of thing is very dangerous," said Tito to his district attorneys. Imagine: everything belongs to these omnipotent regimes—the streets, the cities, the workshops, the factories, everything that is produced. Plus all printing presses, periodicals, and publishing houses. They do not even require censorship, for nothing can be printed that does not suit them. And yet the dictators always tremble anew upon seeing the Medusa face of freedom. How can that be, since they control all the agencies listed above as well as armies, a secret police, and obliging prosecutors? Well, it has been known to happen that even censors themselves grow weak and have to be watched and censored. Even they and the judges may be infected by the ideas whose open utterance they are supposed to prevent.

There are dark phases in history. Not too long ago we lived through them ourselves, we suffered through them day by day. I can still hear the millions of shouts and cries with which Germans triumphantly and menacingly hurled their own servility and bondage in the face of the world. This was dearly paid for—by everyone.

We have since entered a brighter phase. Human history is slowly finding its meaning and purpose again. History would be meaningless if it were not the history of growing, maturing, spreading freedom.

September 1965

P.S. On September 23, 1966, Mihajlov was once more put on trial in Zadar. He had openly voiced his intention of founding a magazine committed to the abolition of the one-party system and to unlimited political and cultural freedom. This time Mihajlov was not alone. A number of intellectuals publicly manifested their solidarity with him, in order thoroughly to investigate and bring into the open the most obtrusive problems. No punishing court of law will be able to prevent them and those like them from doing it.

Fortunes and Misfortunes of Intellectuals in Politics

~~~~~~

E VERY generation resubscribes to three false convictions
that help its insecure egos to survive. The first holds
that anyone who has children is capable of bringing them
up. The second lets each man think he has taste—good taste.
The third, unchallenged, deludes every individual into believing that he can—and should—have his say in politics.

Most people remain indifferent to the major political
problems of the day. Even so, politics thrives from barroom
to ivory tower, with the most frequent type a politics of direct personal interest, incorrectly identified with the politics of one's trade union, corporation, nation—or all mankind. The tendency to declare one's own cause most sacred
and the equivalent claims of others unfair and dangerous
reached its greatest infamy in our century in *sacro egoismo*,

that arrogant avowal of a Mussolini to sacred egotism, and in the formula "Anything useful to the German people is right" or "Whoever opposes the Communist Party is a traitor."

The success of policies determined by "sacred egotism" and paranoiac egocentrism rests in the immediately favorable consensus among the indifferent who are flattered by being told that as craftsmen or technicians, workers or professors, as inhabitants of their city or members of their nation they are unquestionably superior to all outsiders. Naturally, politicians can also evoke the enthusiasm of the indifferent by treating all dissent as criminal and any lack of fulsome agreement as suspicious.

Thus, on the one hand we have an enormous mass of indifferent people, who occasionally put their oars into politics by means of a ballot or other organized and even decreed expression of attitude and who turn away just as quickly. On the other hand we have politicians of many shades and formats. Most of them are local politicians—and there would be nothing to object to if they only resigned themselves to what they are. Generally, however, the spirit of local politics infiltrates national politics, which in turn defines a country's position on world politics. Common sense would naturally have it the other way around, but this narrow-mindedness results from the actual conditions of our everyday life.

We may live in a metropolis, but in point of fact we reside in a certain part of town, a street, a house. We are members of a family rather than of a nation, and the slightest personal or family problem is more urgent than the stormiest problems besetting the life of one's nation or all mankind.

One cannot fully comprehend politics until he has grasped the paradox of this inverse ratio. The larger a framework, the more alien it is to most people; the more limited a context, the closer and greater it appears. My hand is infinitesimally smaller than the cosmos, but placed directly in front of my eyes it covers up the entire world. We are faced with minor politics that confine and delimit all major problems, often distorting them beyond recognition. And, in addition, there exists something that can be labeled "the politics of veiling": private interests use lofty words to evoke universal ideals, morality, and the happiness we wish to ensure for our grandchildren—in short, ideologies of pretext.

But what, beyond all this, is true politics?

Carlo Schmid, who discusses the attitudes of the German educated classes in his volume of essays called *Politik und Geist,* offers this definition:

> Politics is the establishing and preserving of the state; the shaping—loosening and tightening—of its structure; the ordering of relations between various states; but above all, politics is the quality of the individual's relation to the state; politics is the proper commerce with the powers that be, a commerce learned by the cognizing mind and the concern for the people entrusted.

Political activity is obviously manifold and diverse. It comprises administration, organization, diplomacy. It also involves the founding, solidifying, and—if need be— meaningful transforming of the legal bases without which no group can exist. It includes the balancing of opposing interests as well as present and future interests. Finally, it concerns ideas that inspire great actions and are capable of influencing individuals crucially in their relationship to society.

The variety of the entities known as politics easily and frequently makes for confusion in political debate in spite of any striving for objectivity and truth. Considering the nature of these complexities, one might assume that from time immemorial politics has been taught and learned and that essentially people with the proper training ply the trade of politics. Yet the professional politician is a relative innovation.

Even Athenian democracy had no professional politicians. There were, instead, a great number of men who were possessed with politics. The rulers and their cliques had trained helpers, intellectuals who functioned as confidential secretaries, diplomatic couriers, and even father confessors when needed. Primarily, however, these intellectual factotums had to rationalize and defend the deeds and misdeeds of their employers—religiously, morally, and intellectually. They generally refrained from pressing their own policies and concentrated on such politics as suited their employers. In the same spirit, they produced ideologies to demonstrate that the current era was the most meaningful and only possible continuation of the mythical past, and that the future of the regime or dynasty could not be anything but the perpetuation of the present.

Any regime, even the most odious, has always been able to dig up as many obliging intellectuals as it thought it would need: magicians and priests, philosophers and poets, doctors, chemists, jurists. Yet these cerebral assistants have always remained in the wings, becoming visible and vociferous only when permitted or ordered to do so, like court jesters.

The first significant break with this tradition occurred in ancient Israel. The prophets, originally resigning themselves to the function of intellectual gentlemen-in-waiting, made themselves virtually independent. No longer speaking in the name of the king, they spoke for God, who had sent them to preach against the king and his court, against the wickedness of the powerful, the corruption of the rich, even against the unprincipled opportunism of the priests. But, although they invoked the name of God, the prophets were actually the first intellectuals to engage in politics while remaining faithful to their consciences. They had come to carry out a mission; they refused to serve any master or any interest whatsoever.

We know that these men were persecuted and at times even killed cruelly. They loved the people—but in a manner in which nobody cares to be loved. They always reminded the people of unheeded shalt's and shalt-not's and infractions of the Covenant. Relentlessly they demanded good works that would justify each man's existence. They were enemies of the commonplace and scornful of commonplace souls.

In a way, the voice of an Isaiah is still clearly audible. It can be heard wherever men await the kingdom of heaven on earth; wherever men are fighting for a future of liberty, equality, and fraternity. The messianic idea formulated by the prophet Isaiah is still everywhere at work, as is the message that history will come to an end and mankind will finally begin to be itself.

Only a few short centuries after the Hebrew prophet, another great intellectual engaged in politics. Plato went to Syracuse twice, trying to educate a prince in such a way that he could establish once and for all a wise order in the state. Socrates' disciple believed that politics would be sensible and the state guided by a sure hand only if both politics and the state were entrusted to the philosophers. Plato managed to turn a tyrant into a spouter of philosophy, but he never succeeded in making a philosopher into a model ruler. The aging Athenian thinker eventually had to flee for his life. He was captured and would have been sold into slavery if a heavy ransom had not been paid. He was able to return to his Academy in Athens and complete his studies of the philosophical state.

The venture of intellectuals into politics was apparently doomed from the very beginning. Demosthenes' rhetorical gifts have always been lauded, but what did they achieve? Nothing if not the opposite of what he aimed at. And much later, at the onset of the modern age, the last religious intellectual intent on changing the world and establishing the kingdom of heaven on earth, all in the name of God, suffered an ignominious death.

After this event, after Thomas Münzer's defeat, the Revolution spoke a godless language; rather than invoking the Creator, it invoked the will of man—Rousseau's *volonté générale*. And it rejected biblical speech.

> Theory is capable of moving the masses as soon as it is demonstrated *ad hominem,* and it demonstrates *ad hominem* as soon as it becomes radical. Becoming radical means grasping something by its roots. And the root for man is man himself. . . . The critique of religion ends with the teaching that man is the highest being for man, i.e. with the categorical imperative to subvert all conditions in which man is a humiliated, and enslaved, an abandoned, a despised creature.

Thus spoke Karl Marx at the age of twenty-five, a critical follower of Hegel and Ludwig Feuerbach but no less one of the numerous sons of the great French Revolution. This revolution had been the work of a number of people, one might almost say the work of all. Yet it very quickly acquired the character of a highly unusual challenge, the greatest intellectual and spiritual venture since the close of Antiquity. It was the sublime era of dramatic history. Everything unfolded as in a theater in the round; mankind breathlessly followed a spectacle that lasted for years, growing more and more enthralling: its main performers were intellectuals.

This time they did not appear as councilors, father confessors, diplomatic go-betweens, or gray-haired Eminences. They acted as themselves, and they spoke for themselves on behalf of their own consciences for the sake of their own convictions—Robespierre, Camille Desmoulins, Marat, Danton, Saint-Just, and many others. The situation of intellectuals in politics changed completely; the time had come for ideas to play their part in history. These are the words of a German who was nineteen years old when the Bastille was stormed:

> Not since the sun was placed in the firmament and the planets began their revolutions has the like been seen, never before has man stood on his head, i.e. on his mind, and built reality accordingly. . . . A sublime poignancy reigned in that time, an enthusiasm of the *geist* [spirit, mind] thrilled through the world as if this were the first true reconciliation ever to take place between the divine and the world.

With these remarkable and youthful words, Hegel, no longer young, recalled to the Berlin audience of his lectures on philosophy the enthusiasm that had overwhelmed nearly all great intellectuals at the French Revolution—Hegel himself and his friend Hölderlin as well as Klopstock, Schiller, Kant, and many others.

Heretofore it had usually been wars, natural catastrophes, and epidemics that recurrently interrupted the epic course of history and temporarily did away with the everyday world. With the French Revolution history became dramatic, not because of a disaster or a catastrophe independent of human will but as a result of events and decisions all containing one thing in common: the promise of great and ultimate happiness for everyone.

None of the revolutionary leaders had passed his fortieth year; only a very few of them even managed to reach it. The drama was enacted by young intellectuals, and young intellectuals all over the world identified with them. The enthusiasm of which Hegel speaks was thus also the reflection of an extraordinary and extremely long-lasting experience: everyday, commonplace life seemed defeated—forever. The true conciliation of the intellectual and the world was apparently coming about for all to see. Hegel, Hölderlin, and the entire younger generation believed this; even Immanuel Kant, nearing seventy, could not resist the lure of daydreams.

Yet subsequent events squared less and less with the expectation and the promise of happiness. World-conciliating peace did not reign. War raged on all borders. The growing tyranny of the shrinking clique of revolutionaries put an end to freedom. They still spoke as if the great hopes were about to be fulfilled, but the guillotine worked overtime. The revolution committed suicide.

The people got tired of conjugating in the future tense, suffering for the sake of happiness-to-be, so in the end Robespierre and Saint-Just died in utter isolation. A project of intellectuals had failed. Failed? Perhaps not quite. In point of fact, this was in a manner of speaking the most successful defeat humanity has ever suffered. Since the climax of the French Revolution, a hope has been becoming more and more universal—the hope that mankind need not submit to its history as to fate, but that it can shape its own history, fashion it according to its own will. This certitude constitutes the victory of the unvictorious revolution that has endured for 170 years.

But what accounts for the failure of those young intellectuals who for several years had all power in their hands? They beheaded a king, but not—as it turned out—to weaken the state or make the individual freer and more independent. No, at an incredible rate, the Jacobins built a new state more centralized than the *ancien régime*. It identified itself with the nation and thus claimed to be the subject of which the *citoyens,* the members of the state, were to be the predicates. These are not the words of a Saint-Just who engineered a Declaration of the Rights of Man; they were actually spoken by Hegel, albeit only after his enthusiasm for Napoleon had waned and he came to look upon the Prussian state as potentially the universal model of a commonwealth.

The peculiar metamorphosis of revolutionaries who fight for liberty, equality, and fraternity, and then, immediately upon winning, pass all power and privileges over to institutions is one we have experienced in our century. It need not be termed inevitable, yet we can discern that people who go into politics to overhaul the commonwealth in the name of certain ideas far too often terminate their careers as tyrants or as tyrants' henchmen. Granted that every revolution bears in itself counterrevolution as a womb contains an embryo— and that this counterrevolution begins during the day that dawns as the victory of the revolution. We thus come to a first conclusion: The transformation of ideas into institutions as a result of the alliance between the intellectuals (who convey these ideas) and power is responsible for the great disaster intellectuals always experience in politics—the tragic and ironic disaster of becoming one's own enemy and finally adding one more to history's countless false reports concerning fundamental revolutionary changes.

Karl Marx had rejected Hegel's political philosophy at the age of twenty-three precisely because it claimed that the state did not exist for the citizens, but was instead its own goal, and that the citizens served merely as its instruments. We know that in the twentieth century a state, invoking Marxism, came into being and was more absolute than any conservative political philosopher's definitions or dreams.

Two kinds of intellectual involvement in history are clearly distinguishable. One kind occurs in the name of global ideas and ideals. When intellectuals are not fortunate enough to be defeated in time, they become politicians, privileged servants of authority, or even rulers themselves. If so, they actually cease to be intellectuals in politics and are really politicians first and last. As such, they at best practice the art of possibilities and at worst fall prey to the compulsion that rules the powerful: using the most diverse pretexts, they indefatigably have to increase their power. What was originally meant to be a means now turns into an all-determining end that shifts worthy aspirations further and further away and finally consigns them to the unattainable.

The second brand of intellectual activism is fundamental opposition, which strives neither for power nor even for participation. When Voltaire, fighting virtually alone against the infamy of institutions, rose up against the legal violations practiced in the name of religions and law against Chevalier la Barre and the Calas family, the *philosophe* did not pose any political question, he did not even ask about the limits of church power. His indignation was in the name of his own conscience, yet his standpoint was either valid and binding for all men or senseless.

When, some 150 years later, Émile Zola interrupted his work, almost in spite of himself, to take his stand in behalf of the cause of Captain Dreyfus, the Jewish officer who had been sentenced unjustly by a military tribunal, the writer knew very well that he would be enraging the Army, the Church, and all the conformist Frenchmen piously true to the Establishment. Zola was intent on neither a political career nor any involvement in political questions, major or minor. He rose up and gambled everything simply because he could not endure co-existing with the injustice the courts in his country had afflicted upon an innocent man. The novelist sacrificed years of his life to the Dreyfus Affair; he was vilified, persecuted, and finally tried and sentenced to prison. Zola's ultimate victory, which was also a triumph of other great writers including Anatole France, is in my eyes the unassailable and meaningful success intellectuals are meant to strive for. It is their duty to speak up whenever a great injustice—even if the victim is a single individual—threatens to make the citizens of a state or the contemporary world indifferent and unconscionable accomplices of infamy.

Intellectuals have a calling and a *duty* to interfere wherever necessary in order to prevent or pillory certain deeds and whenever a moral or spiritual crisis is about to become a general threat. Voltaire's and Zola's actions have been recalled constantly. We might also mention those of Charles Dickens, Tolstoi, Gorki, Upton Sinclair, Romain Rolland, and of many others closer to us in time.

After the great trial and error of the German revolution of 1848 and the subsequent counterrevolution, the First World War became a fateful acid test that few European intellectuals, particularly those on the Continent, were able to pass. There were even among them some who had once been part of the emancipatory movement of workers and had tirelessly professed opposition to the war. Not forgotten is the manifesto of ninety-four German intellectuals, some of whom, when it was too late, regretted having signed and contritely disavowed it.

> Aren't the connections between art and war metaphorical? I, for one, have always felt that it is not the worst artist who recognizes himself in the image of a soldier. ... We were quite familiar with the world of peace. ... Wasn't it crawling with vermin of the intellect and maggots? Wasn't it rotten and malodorous with the decomposing matter of civilization? ... How could the artist, the soldier in the artist, help but praise God for the collapse of a world of peace he was sick of, so thoroughly sick and tired of. War. We felt catharsis, release, and an enormous optimism. ... Germany's total virtue and

beauty—we now saw it—is fully revealed only in war.
Peace is not always becoming—we occasionally forgot
how beautiful Germany is. . . .

Those words were written by Thomas Mann in the midst
of that war. He continued to regard himself as a non-political and may have considered this stance non-political: "I am
fully convinced that the German people will never be able
to care for political democracy, for the simple reason that
they cannot care for politics itself; the ill-reputed 'authoritarian state' is and always will be the political form best suited
to, and fundamentally desired by, the German people. . . ."
Mann, rightly admired as the most important German
novelist in our time, remained faithful to this concept of au-
thoritarianism later on, even when—during his struggle
against the Nazis and after Hitler's fall—he manifested his
sympathy for totalitarian Stalinism, a sympathy that per-
plexed many of Mann's admirers. He explained his position
in a letter to a Swedish journalist. After pointing out that he
never received any obscene poison-pen letters from the East-
ern zone of Germany and was never attacked there in any
name-calling articles, which was often the case in the West,
he went on to say:
"Is this due only to the threat of Buchenwald—or to a national education, which, more efficacious than in the Western world, takes pains to cultivate respect for an intellectual
being like myself? The authoritarian popular state has its
horrific aspects. But it also includes the boon that stupidity
and impudence at last simply have to shut up. . . ."
Out of respect for the dead writer we will refrain from
commenting on the deliberate or indeliberate naïveté of this
peculiar statement. Besides, any reader will be quite aware
of the possible objections. My aim in quoting these words of
Thomas Mann is to point out that, beyond left-wing or

right-wing ideas, this great intellectual actually always remained true to his "non-political" thinking. Essentially, he
always sided with the well-ordered Establishment. He was no
more a Communist than a National Socialist; he was—if one
may phrase it thus—an "intellectual beast of order." This
instantly brings to mind Goethe's oft-quoted comment that
injustice is preferable to disorder. Goethe was, of course, de-
fending a man he had saved from the counterrevolutionary
mob in Mainz, a mob intent on lynching. But actually,
Goethe, at least after his travels in Italy, also turned into an
"intellectual beast of order." His bearing in the major crises
of his time rarely set a good example.

No century before ours has so frequently and so urgently
laid bare the process by which rebels metamorphose into
counterrevolutionaries. One of the strangest and most signal
cases is certainly that of Bertolt Brecht. From the very out-
set, he acted as a passionately anarchistic and nihilistic spirit.
His best poems, those collected in *Hauspostille,* testify to
this; so do his earliest plays, such as *Drums in the Night.*
Even in *Threepenny Opera,* which made him famous, he
used Gay's *Beggar's Opera* and the verse of François Villon
to hurl a nihilistic challenge in the audience's face. Brecht
then became a Marxist, a Communist. He was the most consistent Stalinist writer who ever wrote. His didactic play
The Measures Taken was one long encomium of the unlimited villainy of the GPU and, remarkably enough, of the
Moscow trials Stalin was to stage a few years later.

In his play Brecht "proved" that it is a capital crime to
follow the dictates of one's own conscience, preserve one's
own will, and do the right thing without the orders of Moscow's Central Committee. This was the Stalinist axiom,
which Brecht eloquently anticipated: the right thing does
not exist without orders. Herbert Lüthy, who in his volume
of essays *Nach dem Untergang des Abendlandes (After the*

Decline of the West) uses those words to sum up the quintessence of Brecht's play, also answers the question how and why Brecht became the Bard of the totalitarian party. "It wasn't the worker's movement (it had never interested him); it wasn't revolutionary communism (he was unacquainted with it); it was the new Byzantium that attracted him, the rigidly hierarchical state-church founded on the infallibility of the head; it wasn't *the idea,* it was *organization as a self-purpose,* naked power-technique as the grand framework and model of a somber and sacred masque."

Incredible as it may sound, even Brecht could to a certain extent have claimed that his thinking was actually non-political. This world-famous Communist never became a member of the Communist Party. Fleeing from the German invasion of his asylum in Denmark in 1940, he landed in Finland, just a few miles away from the "Fatherland of Socialism," the land of his desire. But he was always an expert at curbing his desire; he sought refuge, not in the nearby Soviet Union but in faraway California. After the war, this native of Augsburg, Germany, acquired Austrian citizenship before settling in the Soviet sector of Berlin. The contradictions in his behavior were partly explicated in his extremely clever play about Galileo.

Although raising their voices to point out a way, neither of the two great German writers mentioned belonged to the tribe of prophetic ideologists, for even their short-lived rebellion was conformist—in accord with some state or other, its institutions, its Establishment, its power.

Yet Bertolt Brecht, as opposed to Thomas Mann, was a master of the "swivel-eye." Many intellectuals learned from him how to make decisions based on prior opinions of the Party when telling right from wrong and Cain from Abel. Naturally, the swivel-eyed have always existed, the devoted ideologists of the powerful. Today, some of them are even self-styled revolutionaries and side with the torturers when their victims belong to the opposite camp, yet energetically protest against even the slightest limitations on freedom if they themselves or their partisans are at stake. This would simply be a customary partisan narrow-mindedness—if these swivel-eyed souls refrained from invoking ethics and thereby degrading basically sound reasons into mere pretexts.

To take an example: These swivel-eyed souls considered it perfectly proper that even opponents of communism should take up the cause of the French-Algerian Communist Henri Alegh and the circulation of his book against the torture used on the FLN and its members. Yet these same souls found nothing wrong with the fact that Alegh supported the Ulbricht regime in the Soviet zone of Germany or that he never said a word against the imprisonment of the intellectuals rotting in Ulbricht's jails because of their dissident political views.

In contrast let me cite the example of a French typographer and journalist named Louis Lecoin.

Lecoin was born in the Auvergne in 1888, the son of penniless dirt-farmers. At sixteen he settled in Paris, instantly entering a circle of socialists and anarchists. Three years later he served his first prison sentence for conspicuously agitating in a truck farmer's strike.

A year later, during his hitch in the Army, he was sentenced again, this time for refusing to take part in action against striking railroad workers. Two years later he was condemned to five years in prison for disseminating pacifist propaganda. No sooner was he released than he profited from his freedom to write, print, and circulate flyers entitled *Let's Get Peace by Using Force.* He was arrested and sentenced to five years, as well as to eighteen months for his courageous actions in court. The judge simply could not shut him up as Lecoin unrelentingly attacked the government and all the belligerent nations. After four years' incarceration, he was pardoned. But only one year later, he initiated an action in favor of political prisoners. He was sentenced anew and began his first hunger strike. He endured a second one shortly thereafter to force a lighter sentence for Jeanne Morand, a condemned anarchist. As publisher of the anarchist gazette *Libertaire,* he became one of the most active leaders of the campaign for releasing the Spaniards Ascaso, Durutti, and Jover. With utmost energy he took up the cause of Sacco and Vanzetti and was at the head of the hundreds of thousands of Parisians who poured through the streets in 1927, demanding justice for the two Italian anarchists.

When the Civil War broke out in Spain, Louis Lecoin founded a Committee for Free Spain, which later called itself *Solidarité Internationale Antifasciste* and is still in existence. It was one of the few organizations on the Republican side that did not promote Stalinism and that supported the liberty and welfare of the Spanish people with no ulterior motives whatsoever. Once more, Lecoin was fighting for peace and freedom, devoting all his strength and all his being to the cause. During all these years he remained a typographer and never went into politics professionally.

Lecoin is an integral—unconditional—pacifist, for which he had to endure still more years in prison. But it was only through his final action that he became famous throughout the world, at least the Free World.

In his tiny proletarian apartment in the slums of Paris, the seventy-four-year-old man began an action that was perilous and could easily have proved fatal for him. He went on a hunger strike that lasted for twenty-two days, from June 1 to June 22, 1962. He did this to force passage of a French law in favor of conscientious objectors. The old man was not fighting for himself or for his sons or grandsons. It was not the struggle of a man who demands a privilege for his own conscience while denying others the very same privilege. Lecoin is not a religious man; since his youth he has been a free-thinker. Yet without the least hesitation he fought for Jehovah's Witnesses, a Christian sect that claims conscientious objection. And he fought for all those who—whatever their ideology—are driven by genuine qualms of conscience to choose the path of resistance against the state. Louis Lecoin terminated his hunger strike on the twenty-second day only because the government and President de Gaulle promised him that his demands would be fulfilled and that the military would recognize conscientious objection. He also demanded that the several hundred young men who had been jailed for refusing to serve in the armed forces would be set at liberty.

The promises were kept in part, but it took fifteen months for this old man, acting almost alone in France, to help establish the right to refuse military service for reasons of conscience.

Here we have the case of a man who does not dream of exchanging one authoritarian Establishment for another and who has never become the accomplice of injustice. As an antimilitarist he opposes all wars; if he is against the persecution of the innocent, he takes up their causes no matter what ideology the persecutors may invoke. He has no double-entry system of bookkeeping; his morality has no double standard.

The postwar world has witnessed the growth of a kind of specialized pacifism that is especially widespread among intellectuals. I am referring to the organized opponents of nuclear arms. Primarily in England, but also in Germany and other free countries, these intellectuals organize Easter and Pentecost marches and other conspicuous demonstrations against the production, storage, and certainly the use of

atomic weapons. Many people might even think that these intellectuals have met with success, for obviously the two
world powers, America and Russia, are definitely afraid of
atomic war. This fear, however, is not the result of philanthropic sermons or antinuclear books and articles, Easter or
Pentecost marches, conferences or congresses of antinuclear
intellectuals; it is simply a consideration of the destructive
power of the giant H-bombs. The latter have wiped away
any illusion that either of the two powers could possibly conquer the other and live to enjoy its victory.

What we *are* dealing with is a sort of moral rebellion, and
so the matter is quite a serious one. It is perfectly fair for
people to feel called upon to shape public opinion, to raise
their voices in warning—and to do so without making any
personal allowances and in disregard of any tactical, strategic, partisan, or ideological opportunism.

Let us pause to consider the case of the spiritual leader of
these antinuclear strugglers, that impressive old man Bertrand Russell. One of the most remarkable lone-wolf intellectuals in our century, Russell has often changed his views,
and no one could possibly hold it against him. Thus, at the
end of World War II, he was an energetic opponent of the
Soviet Union. He pilloried Stalinist methods and went so far
as to declare that after wiping out Fascism, the United States
should annihilate the Soviet regime. He accordingly demanded that America threaten the Soviets with, and even
use, the atomic bomb in order to bring them to their knees.

The very same Bertrand Russell came out for and still
supports unilateral and unconditional nuclear disarmament
in the Western world. In October 1962, when President
Kennedy gave Khrushchev the well-known Cuba Ultimatum,
Lord Russell claimed that Kennedy's accusations were
trumped up and that the Russians had not constructed any
missile base in Cuba. Russell and his adherents conducted a

ferocious propaganda campaign against the United States right in the middle of the Russian-caused Cuba crisis, all in the name of pacifism. Russell demanded that Kennedy be tried as a war criminal.

Once again we come upon a case of swivel-eyes, which makes the moral legitimacy of certain antinucleists questionable—to say the least. The self-righteousness of these inconsistently Draconian moralists is effectively promoted by the antinuclear cant.

Before stating my position, I would like to insert a personal remark. Between my ninth and eleventh year, I witnessed war from nearly the same distance as a soldier on the front. I saw people killing and dying. To a prematurely aware child both seemed senseless—nay, insane and despicable, like any violent weakness. Nothing on earth is as hateful to me as war, no matter how sublime the rationale may be, no matter what weapons are involved. In short, I am not finicky with regard to lethal weapons and I am no mathematician when it comes to despising murder. Any firearm is too much for me; the fate of a single soldier who has died in action is, in my eyes, a defeat for all other human beings who tolerate the killing of one innocent man by another long before the victim's time has come.

High statistics do not impress me. In this century of world wars and the death camps of Hitlers and Stalins, the population of our planet has multiplied at a rapidly growing rate; it is the *in*crease and not *de*crease of the inhabitants of earth that will pose an alarming and even inconceivably dangerous problem by the year 2000. This fruitfulness will have deadly consequences if we do not manage quickly to increase, and profit from, atomic energy through nuclear fission and fusion.

For industrial society in 1960, which comprises only a fraction of humanity, the available sources of energy are more than enough. They are far from enough, however, to raise billions of human beings to the level of industrial society within a few decades and really "naturalize" them in our century. Only the unlimited release of atomic energy offers a fearfully prolific mankind the solution to survival.

A new era began not with Hiroshima, not even with the thermonuclear bombs; it began with the atomic-energy centers that transform unfertile land and deserts into thriving fields and gardens, that obtain sweet water from salt sea, and that will ultimately do away with the problem of location for industrial production. Atomic energy will terminate prehistory, perhaps even before the end of the century, and make possible a transition from a world of enslaving material necessity to a world of freedom from all material need.

Any normal person hates death and certainly mass murder. It is safe to say that the feverish atomic rearmament of the two world powers before Stalin's death has postponed a third world war, probably making it impossible forever; we can hope that in the foreseeable future war will die because of atomic weapons. The crucial thing, however, is that for thousands of years mankind has been using the destructive energy discovered and invented constructively and not self-destructively; *men create more than they destroy; conditions are stronger than events; procreation is faster than death.* During the last war, in the midst of profound despair, I placed these words in the mouth of a hero in one of my novels. Hiroshima has not altered their truth.

The antinuclear cant, questionable and unpleasant like any cant, is—despite its overdramatizing of frequently genuine, occasionally fictitious turmoil of conscience—the sentimental expression of a thoroughly decent conviction. But convictions no longer suffice in politics. One has the right to demand of intellectuals that they choose their positions on the basis of knowledge, insight, and awareness.

So as not to leave the reader with the impression that the role of intellectuals in politics is insignificant, or that their activities are doomed to failure, or that their protests and wishes are nonsense, I would like to state expressly that non-intellectual politicians, especially in our century, have far too often been blind to the most important facts and trends; in the setting of goals and the choice of means they have so often failed miserably that a person would have to be inadmissibly foolish or politically innocent to regard the failures and misfortunes of intellectuals gone astray in politics or acting upon ulterior motives as proof of a political imcompetence endemic to them alone.

Our goal is to outline the broad relationship between ideology and politics.

The current usage of the word *ideology* is relatively new and in a way incorrect—especially since for the past sixty years it has been the Marxists, and particularly the Communists, who have brought it into fashion. For Karl Marx and Friedrich Engels as well as for their closer friends and disciples—these "Doctors of the Revolution," as Heinrich Heine called them—the term *ideology* had a bad tinge to it. It meant an abstruse hodgepodge of confused ideas, useless abstractions that muddled heads viewed as reality instead of investigating reality to acquire testable knowledge and gain insight into the true conditions of society. Marxists spoke pejoratively of the "politicaster" ideologists; Marx and Engels attacked them in their giant pamphlet *The Holy Family* and in *German Ideology*. Neither Marx nor Engels considered himself an ideologist; they viewed themselves as social scientists, revolutionaries who emerged in the historical situation in which the goals of utopian socialism were scientifically graspable and able to come true: the millennium of necessity was nearing its end. Their "scientific socialism" was about to lead mankind into the millennium of freedom.

Unlike Hegel, they were determined to take the world the ideologists had turned topsy-turvy and to place it right-side-up.

Ideology is more than ever before a favorite topic of conversation, and now it means essentially a total system embracing the world, mankind, the present situation, the problems of the times, the possibilities and necessities in all their ramifications, making all these factors understandable and at the same time serving as a guide for all followers to the final goal.

Thus, if an important philosopher like Jean-Paul Sartre pledged himself to Marxism, at least politically and in opposition to his metaphysics, he did so because he felt that Communist ideology offered a total political system that compressed all programs into a single one and promised to solve them all totally. From this viewpoint we can understand why men such as Sartre or a highly intelligent writer like Brecht were both drawn to and repelled by the totalitarian regime. Both men believed that its inhumanity matched the giant yardstick of human problems and could therefore offer a method to solve immediately and once and for all the entire lot of mankind's social problems.

The enormous deception of a final and total solving of all questions is at the heart of any ideology of mass movements whose victory has led to a totalitarian regime. Anyone who joined, and submitted himself, was possessed of an unassailable certainty that he now understood everything better than those who were not part of the movement and that he and his peers were following the only possible route to the only desirable and irrevocable solution. The totalitarian ideologies managed to infiltrate the civilized nations because terrible and completely senseless wars as well as devastating and degrading crises had brought about widespread despair, the kind that seeks salvation only in illusory and total hopes and therefore sacrifices the intellect, i.e., all independent thinking.

These ideologies are rooted in the nineteenth century; but only our age has tested them, lived and killed for them, and died *en masse* for them. They are virtually a secular messianism, a godless religion of mass murder, a utopia running amok.

The political ideologist does not ask, "What is possible? What can we attain today or tomorrow with the least expenditure of means and victims?" He really demands the immediate realization of his goal. He never worries about the cost to human life; for him no stake is too huge.

Politics as the art of the possible is neither apocalyptic nor messianic. It limits itself to its own goals and in the choice of means. It knows that there are victories that should not be forced because the price would be vastly out of proportion to the value and the destruction equivalent to that of defeat.

It knows that a compromise—albeit despised by so many intellectuals and nonintellectuals, by rebels and prattlers—is usually the best solution to difficult problems because it will elicit neither too great a regret nor dangerous resentment. The art of the possible is thus wiser and more humane than any politics inspired by ideology.

The truth of the matter is that this self-moderating politics can be good and wise only when conditions are more or less normal, when problems are not completely new, and conflicts not extreme. In the thirties, the Western powers tried such a politics with Hitler and fifteen years later they followed suit with Stalin. In both cases the blunder was catastrophic.

It is not true that indifference to expansive violence and reckless injustice is humane and wise; no one has the right to shut his eyes and ears to these things when the rules of human relations are arbitrarily and violently disregarded. And this is why intellectuals, at least since Isaiah, have always had an important and unavoidable task to carry out: they have to warn and reiterate in the fight against the perils and lures of power and against the narrow-mindedness of so-called *Realpolitik,* which fails to acknowledge the ephemerality of its conquests simply because it views the present as the omnipotent heir to the past rather than as the past of the future.

October 1965

Charles De Gaulle, the Vanquished Victor

THE most ominous of the many contradictions manifest in our century involves the value and the role of the individual in the constantly accelerating process of social change. As early as World War I, the fighting soldiers, frantically celebrated as heroes, were further and further devalued as individuals, finally melting into a mass of faceless cannon-fodder, "unprecedented human sacrifices ..." As hundreds of thousands of young Europeans mechanically murdered one another in a matter of days and sometimes even hours, the individual lost his most important and most inviolable privilege: the right to be himself. He became an anonymous particle of "human material," as the term went, which first had to die to be honored in memorial speeches.

The more insignificant the individual became, the more power accrued to the generals, who were totally incapable of fighting that war. They had prepared themselves and their armies for traditional battles which, after the first few weeks, proved impossible to manage. The mobile war got out of hand; it was, so to speak, buried in the trenches: the spade that had been used to shovel up mounds of earth as a shield against concentrated gunfire interred the traditional art of war practiced by the generals. Their undeserved praises were sung more and more loudly, as the victims of their ineptness piled up at a horrifying rate.

Soon after the war there were signs that mankind was ashamed of its military enthusiasm and homicidal hatred, and regretted its passion for heroes. This regret, however, was short-lived. Major economic crises and the resulting deep transformations once again degraded the individual into a particle in the mass, a member of a gigantic cast of obedient extras offering themselves as builders of the destiny of their nation, if not of all humanity. The higher a Hitler or Stalin climbed, the more worthless the individual became. This was the continuation of the moral and political decay that had begun in World War I.

Charles De Gaulle was shaped by his experiences in that war. The ideas that determined his path and contributed to his eventual ascent are comprehensible only within the context of the permanent catastrophe of 1914–1918.

We are familiar with different interpretations of history: religious, moral, economic, technological, and dynastic ones, heroistic and racist ones, not to mention their countless variations.

At school we usually learn the history of our own nation as if it were the heart of the world, in accordance with a heroist approach. Past history appears virtually as a collective biography of allegedly or truly great men. All the good things about their lifetimes and reigns are attributed to them, and sometimes even the bad things. If a great man is not so much a dynastic ruler as a general, a successful statesman, a usurper, or a dictator, then the enormously consequential changes that took place in his time are praised or attacked as exclusively his doing.

Obviously, anyone interested in history is in search of dramatic events depicted so grippingly as to make one feel that one was present at moments of destiny. And obviously developments and decisions in the lives of individuals and groups tend to be dramatic and eventful. However . . .

I, for one, regard the heroizing and the dramatic approach to history as false and deceptive, and prefer a narrative approach instead. The gradual or accelerated development of conditions and circumstances in which men live and multiply, create lasting works, develop techniques of ferreting out nature's secrets, is the history of man, the history of civilization. The dramatic event per se is merely the means by which obsolete conditions are replaced by innovations, which must sooner or later be digested and assimilated.

This statement of belief in the basically narrative character of human history is necessary simply because Charles De Gaulle is a downright melodramatic phenomenon. His rise in the midst of a world crisis and a national catastrophe, his return to power, his special mastery of politics make him an ideal hero for a heroizing and dramatic conception of history. Furthermore, De Gaulle, with all his considerable gifts as a writer and speaker, always makes an effective stage appearance.

The skeptical narrative historian is always aware that nothing began with us and that nothing will end with us, that there will not be any end. This realization is comforting or highly discouraging—it all depends—but in any event it protects us from the enticements of the moment, which is megalomaniacal precisely because it already and still is present. Thanks to this view we can illuminate the three tenses as a single continuum of time, in which lies and legends fare badly.

The contemporaries of Hitler and Stalin have not forgotten how greatly both the present *and* the future appeared to depend on those supermen who thought themselves strong enough to change even the past. In their hands mankind seemed like a moldable material, merely clay on the potter's wheel. Their whims were commands to be immediately carried out. And the resulting action, so they thought, determined the course of history for centuries, for a millennium. But now these potters are dead and denounced,—more ephemeral, more *past* than clay that has dropped from the potter's hand.

To avoid any misunderstanding, Charles De Gaulle is not comparable to either of these two, nor to Mussolini nor any other dictator of the last few decades. He *does* have a strong sense of power and an almost untamable will to command, but these traits determine neither his essential character, nor his plans and projects, nor his actions. One could best liken him to Leon Trotsky; like Trotsky before the Russian revolution, De Gaulle had a clear idea of the part he wanted to play long before the collapse of France. He had a well-founded conception of the course of history and the way he wanted to influence it.

Ever since his early youth, De Gaulle had been preparing to play a part, if possible a leading role, in the life of the *grande nation*. He waited impatiently for his cue to enter.

And the moment came. He transformed his highly personal, subjective idea of the future into a political and ultimately a historical reality. The start of this fateful change can be precisely dated June 18, 1940. Charles De Gaulle was fifty years old; the impatient man had waited a quarter of a century for his cue.

"As the irrevocable words fled, I felt a life coming to a close within me—the life I had led in a secure France and an indivisible army. . . . I embarked on the adventure like a man whom Destiny has flung from all hierarchies."

With the above words, De Gaulle describes his act—that radio speech of June 18—which was to transform a career officer into a mutineer, and thus into a strange and at first ambiguous historical figure.

Scarcely ten years after that evening De Gaulle withdrew daily to his tower, the tower he had built near his country house in the village of Colombey-les-deux Églises, to lock himself up in privacy. He refused to believe that his career was over or that his part in French and international politics was played out. It was in that tower that he wrote his three-volume work entitled *War Memoirs*—not so much to tell posterity what he had experienced, done, and prevented, as to continue and perfect his actions by another means. He was determined that coming generations should see him and his actions as he did.

We have a rough idea of the biography of Charles André Marie Joseph De Gaulle (born in Lille on November 22, 1890), a charismatic Frenchman who at the age of fifty began to live as if he were a legend come true, and who is now the President of the Fifth Republic, which exists only because he contributed almost as much to the death of the Fourth Republic as to the birth of the Fifth.

Anyone reading a newspaper or listening to the radio in any of the five continents is bound to come upon his name. He is a man who for years has been continuously causing talk. And he likes to cause it.

Now, upon finishing his seventy-fifth year of life, rather than looking back he is intent on determining the future direction of France, perhaps of Europe, preferably of the whole world. Not only Europeans are wondering with concern what De Gaulle's next move will be. "Will he really destroy the Common Market? Does he want to degrade it to a *quantité négligeable?* Will he really leave NATO? Is he sincerely after an alliance with Russia—at the expense of Germany, Western Europe and the whole Free World?" Perhaps some of De Gaulle's confidants could answer these questions. But it is just as conceivable that De Gaulle himself does not know the answers.

An example may help to explain such a doubt. From summer, 1965, to the evening of November 4, 1965, all Frenchmen, from De Gaulle's closest colleagues to ordinary newspaper readers, were asking themselves whether he would run for the presidency or not. No small number of his admirers and the majority of his opponents were convinced that the General had made up his mind long ago and was keeping his decision secret for tactical reasons only—and perhaps to achieve a theatrical effect as well. And it *is* true that in every situation De Gaulle is intent on producing the greatest effect. Nevertheless, there are good reasons to think that he actually did waver in those months, and assigned himself a deadline for the decision. This coolly reflective, calculating, power-conscious politican has been living in the shadow of old age for years, in the ceaselessly oppressive, painful awareness that his fall will come sooner or later, inevitable and irresistible. He was afraid, and will remain afraid until the end, that as his own successor he would become a caricature of himself, that during the seven years, in the last of which he would be eighty-two, he might stumble mortally or, even worse, ridiculously over the insuperable obstacle of accumulated years.

Such intelligent, rational considerations should have induced him to retire at the end of his seven-year mandate; but his rationality conceals a strange, irrational belief:

"All my life I have formed a certain image of France, an image based on feeling and intelligence. To my feelings, France always seemed like the king's daughter in a fairy tale or the Madonna in mural frescoes: destined to a sublime and extraordinary fate. I instinctively have the impression that providence has destined France for perfect fortune or exemplary misfortune."

These words preface the 2,000 pages of De Gaulle's three-volume war memoirs; they are the first words of the first volume. The final words of the last volume are: "In the face of the world that looks upon us, we want to rebuild France."

In French, France is called *la France.* This word need not refer to a land or a realm; it could just as easily be a woman's name. Frenchmen often speak of *la douce France,* "gentle, sweet, tender France." One cannot conceive of a writer of memoirs less sentimental than De Gaulle but the moment he speaks of *la France,* the attentive reader discovers an ardent burst of feeling, the only one the author never seems to eschew.

We have only superficial knowledge of the personal experiences, relationships, and character traits of this important contemporary, who has written so much about himself without ever exposing himself, who so stubbornly puts himself center stage, makes a star of himself, as Frederick the Great wanted to, while at the same time keeping complete control of the lighting and special effects. Besides De Gaulle, so many of his friends and foes, his admirers and detractors have written about him—and yet he remains one of the least known people in modern history. The French *bon mot, un illustre inconnu*—an unknown celebrity—describes him to a T. In one of his rare personal utterances about himself he has admitted: "As far as my personal relationships go, my fate is loneliness."

Henri De Gaulle, whose second son was Charles, came from an old Parisian family, but not from the grand aristocracy of those De Gaulles occasionally mentioned in French history. General De Gaulle's father was an administrative official, and later a teacher of literature and philosophy at a Jesuit *lycée* in Paris. Untoward material circumstances had prevented him from following a military career. The De Gaulles had been lower officials for generations, more infrequently officers or clergymen. Charles De Gaulle's mother, Jeanne Maillot, came from a middle-class family in Lille; she returned to her native city to give birth to her second son in her parental home.

The family was, in accordance with its station, Catholic, royalist, and extremely patriotic; Henri De Gaulle's five children learned that *la France* was the most admirable work that forty French kings had produced in a millennium. The well-bred children never doubted that the French Army, despite the terrible defeat of 1870, was one "of the greatest phenomena in the world," as Charles De Gaulle would often reiterate afterwards.

It was probably from his father that Charles inherited a passion for history and the boundless diligence with which he began carefully memorizing knowledge at an early age, much as one learns by heart a poem that one admires. And the old man is still a memorizer. He still carefully stylizes all his speeches with great care and then doughtily commits them to memory. It may be that he also rehearses the awkward gestures of his very long arms, which so often underscore his words at press conferences.

Naturally he went to a Catholic school, the Lycée Sainte Geneviève, rather than to a state—i.e., secular—school. Then he became a cadet at St. Cyr, where he was conspicuous because of his excessive height and nicknamed "double meter."

When the cadets put on plays, they assigned him comic parts, one good reason being the enormous nose in the tiny face above the gigantic body. We may assume that the young man suffered all the more because of his appearance since he had set himself lofty goals at a very early age.

It was in school that he began to write; a verse play won

an award and was published in a provincial review. It was entitled *A Bad Encounter,* and the hero was a rather unhappy bandit. The officer-to-be had earnestly read all the authors fashionable in his milieu: Barrès, Déroulède, Rostand. They and others like them express French chauvinism in all their works, and quite a number of them were obsessed by the idea of France's reconquering Alsace-Lorraine. The thought of an imminent war was a familiar feeling for De Gaulle from earliest youth, and the Dreyfus Affair, which had stirred up the country almost to the point of civil war, remained topical. In contrast to those around him, Charles De Gaulle's father was not anti-Dreyfus; he may have lost his position in the police prefecture for voicing doubts as to the Jewish captain's guilt.

One of the thinkers most strongly influencing the future general was Charles Péguy, an open-minded Catholic writer, around whose magazine *Les Cahiers de la quinzaine* the best minds rallied. De Gaulle was probably also influenced by the royalist extremist Charles Maurras and by the philosopher-psychologist Henri Bergson, who exerted a hard-to-explain influence on the French upper classes and the leaders of the Army.

When World War I broke out, Charles De Gaulle was twenty-four years old. He was prepared mentally and psychologically as well as militarily. What he wrote about the Army's attitude held for him, too:

"Calm, imbued with an unuttered hope, the Army was waiting for the moment when everything would depend on it."

A lieutenant in the 33rd Infantry Regiment, commanded by Philippe Pétain, De Gaulle spent the summer of 1914 filled with expectancy:

"France will have to endure powerful trials, and the interest of life will consist in someday performing an important service for France. From now on the opportunity will be presenting itself."

Later, after the baptism by fire, he was to talk about military action as a divine heroic drama.

De Gaulle actually did fight courageously and was wounded three times, the third time at Douaumont in 1916, where he passionately led his company in a storm attack. He was thought to be lost. The division report praised and lamented him as an incomparable officer. But he had only been wounded and made prisoner.

Naturally he tried to escape several times before he was finally brought to Fort IX in Ingolstadt. The POW camp became a kind of school of continuing education for him. He pursued his historical studies and learned German, and read German newspapers daily. These readings inspired a piece that he first published in 1924, entitled *Discord in the Enemy*. It is notable that this career officer pointed out, in his first book, that a country is greatly in danger if ambitious officers, particularly during a war, gain the upper hand over statesmen and, instead of obeying, make political decisions themselves. This piece was primarily aimed at Ludendorff, whose intrigues in 1917 led to the ousting of Chancellor Bethmann-Hollweg.

In 1919 De Gaulle was put at the service of the Polish Army. Good pupil that he was, he industriously learned Polish and surprised his listeners by giving his memorized speeches partly in Polish. In the summer of 1920, the Red Army invaded Poland and marched toward Warsaw; De Gaulle joined an active unit. He must have greatly distinguished himself, for he was awarded the *Virtuti Militari,* the highest Polish decoration.

A year after his return from Poland, De Gaulle, promoted to captain, married Yvonne Verdoux, a daughter of the middle class in Calais. The couple settled in Paris, in the very same district where he had grown up, albeit in a very modest apartment. He became an auxiliary teacher, first in St. Cyr, and then in the École Militaire, France's military academy. After a while, he once more became a student and prepared for the entrance examination at the so-called Troisième Bureau. He failed to get straight As, without which no one was admitted to this strategic study division of the general staff. Prior to the test, his teachers characterized him as follows:

"Intelligent, educated, serious officer. Brilliant, with great substance. Unfortunately he spoils his indisputable assets by his exaggerated self-assurance, his rigorous attitude towards other people's opinions, and his behaving like a king in exile."

One can admire the psychological acumen of these teachers, and note with no surprise that the old President of 1958 and the thirty-four-year-old captain of 1924 are alike as two peas in a pod.

After his failure he was to return to the Army, in Mainz. But a man intervened, a man who was to play a unique and contradictory role in De Gaulle's life. Philippe Pétain, initially commander of the 33rd Infantry Regiment, later divisional chief, and eventually Army general of the front sections in which De Gaulle fought, developed an early interest in this officer, whose very outward appearance was conspicuous and whose disarmingly precise and unusual historical knowledge always made him stand out in discussions. It was Marshal Pétain who saw to it that De Gaulle might return to Paris and give lectures at the École Militaire. In his talks there, he developed ideas that were to influence his mind and his career in the course of time. These ideas involved the specific tasks of the officer at the head of his troops and more generally the psychology of the commander:

People destined for struggles, trials, and great things do not always reveal those easily recognizable qualities, those pleasing traits that are so popular in the ordinary course of life. Strongly marked characters are normally unapproachable, uncomfortable, nay, harsh.

The man of character embodies in his own person the rigor necessary for great exertions. Furthermore, such a leader maintains a certain distance, for authority is not possible without prestige, nor prestige without distance. A grumbling will arise about his arrogance and his demands. But when he acts, criticism will fade.

He wrote the above later on, in 1932, in *Le Fil de l'épée* (*The Sword's Edge*). But he was also interested in an accelerated motorization of the army. He particularly advocated the formation of large, operatively independent tank units. He was not the only postwar military thinker looking for ways to make the fronts mobile, to "pull the war back out of the earth," as he put it. De Gaulle concluded that the draft army had to be replaced by a new, highly specialized professional army.

For quite a while, Pétain seemed favorable to De Gaulle's efforts toward a renovation of the Army and strategy. He gave him a position in his staff—the Marshal was vice-president of the Supreme War Council and General Inspector of the Army. Sometimes he would introduce his colleague with, "Gentlemen, listen attentively to Captain De Gaulle, for the day will come when a grateful France will summon him."

These words were spoken on April 7, 1927, thirteen years before the omnipotent head of state Pétain demoted the mutinous Brigadier General De Gaulle, condemned him to death in absentia, and stripped him of French citizenship.

That lies ahead of us, however; we are still in the year 1927. Pétain is a republican Marshal; his protégé is off to Trèves, where he advances to the rank of major and commands a battalion of occupation troops. Around this time, De Gaulle writes prophetic words to his friend Nachin:

"The way to power depends on smashing down all the traditional and partially valuable fences still existing in Europe. We have to assume that the annexation of Austria is not far off and that Germany, with or without the use of violence, will re-appropriate everything it was forced to yield to Poland. And after that, she will demand Alsace back from us. All this is clearly written in the sky."

These words were written in 1928, five years before Hitler came to power. On June 20, 1929, De Gaulle wrote the following strange lines to the same friend:

"Oh, how bitter it is to wear military garb in these days. And yet we must. In a few years people will be begging us to save the fatherland as well as the rabble."

One could quote many more written and spoken utterances of De Gaulle's, eloquently testifying to his acumen. Naturally, those biographers desirous of setting up a monument to him are particularly zealous in ferreting out such texts. When one wishes to laud the prescience of a person, one quotes mainly what has already come true. The rest is forgotten or neglected.

De Gaulle did not remain in Trèves for long. He left Germany and Europe, and took study trips to Syria, Lebanon, and other colonial areas. Upon returning to Paris, he was assigned to the General Secretariat of the Supreme Council of National Defense. It was then that his real writing career began. He published the above-mentioned *Le Fil de l'épée*, in a sense the most complete presentation of his main ideas. One may assert that between 1940 and 1946, but particularly after his return to power in June 1958, he began to realize, if not to embody, these ideas.

In 1934, he published his plea for a professional army, which was generally rejected by both officers and politicians.

The inaccessibly haughty De Gaulle became his own p.r. man, haunting the offices of editors to win over military specialists to his ideas and get articles printed in which he might present his argument to a wider audience.

At the same time, he methodically sought the acquaintanceship of parliamentary delegates, senators, party leaders, and ministers, to whom he submitted oral and written exposés proving the necessity of immediate independent armored units if not armored armies.

Naturally these ideas were not as original as they were subsequently thought to be by some people. When General Von Seeckt created the professional army of the Weimar Republic he thought of using the most modern technological means to multiply the potential of a hundred thousand troops. As for armored divisions, we know that the French general Estienne, the Austrian Eimannsberger, whom Guderian cites, and finally the latter himself, as well as a number of others, recognized the strategic importance of tanks.

As of 1933 at the latest, De Gaulle concentrated all his energy on warning France of the imminent war; he tirelessly demanded that the French army be materially, strategically, and tactically prepared for the dreadful trial. He was not alone, for in the later Minister President Paul Reynaud he found an intelligent, influential follower and protector. But the leaders of the French Army lost all interest in him. Even Pétain turned his back on him.

The reason for the coolness between Pétain and De Gaulle was ridiculous and disappointing for both. In 1938, De Gaulle put out a book, *France and Her Army,* for which he had begun collecting material while still in Pétain's cabinet. It may be true that the Marshal inspired him, or wanted to deal with the theme himself, asking his colleague to put a file together. When the book was about to appear, De Gaulle sent his former boss the brush-proofs and asked his approval for form's sake. The Marshal's reaction was unexpected; he demanded that he himself be named as initiator and inspirer. De Gaulle refused; this caused a rupture which could have come about much sooner, and for far more cogent, nonpersonal reasons. Like General Weygand, Pétain advocated that the French Army be drilled in defensive tactics, and that a protective wall in north-east France replace the trenches of World War I. France's soldiers would slip into the cells of the so-called Maginot Line until the enemy's defensive and fire had worn themselves out on it. In a preface to a book entitled *Is Invasion Still Possible?* Pétain stressed that neither the air force nor the tank would play an important part in a coming war. This position would have sufficed to estrange the two men, since Pétain in any case had a growing aversion to De Gaulle, who seemed downright suspicious for allying himself with Republican politicians and even seeking the approval of Socialist Deputies. Thus he tried to win over Léon Blum and other men of the Popular Front, which had come to power in 1936. De Gaulle's behavior appeared unreliable to the officers' corps, and his refusal to express gratitude to his superior in his book seemed highly inelegant. But things became even worse:

In January 1940, De Gaulle passed out a memorandum to eighty of the most important people in the country, demanding that the responsible politicians force the army leaders to immediately change their strategy—in line with the conception he had been hawking for years. It was in this unfavorable light that De Gaulle's desperate attempts were presented to a Gamelin or a Georges.

Paul Reynaud, having become Premier, made De Gaulle Undersecretary of State in the War Ministry, bringing him back from the front, where De Gaulle had been provisionally promoted to brigadier general, and was commanding the IVth Division. We know (a great deal has been written about it) that he sent his tanks into action near Laon on the seventeenth and nineteenth of May. Guderian describes it in his memoirs; he recalls that De Gaulle's tanks came within a mile and a half of his headquarters.

Between May 28 and 30, De Gaulle was moved to Abbeville, where he overcame enemy positions and took 400 prisoners; but after two days he had to withdraw. He never returned to the front, in fact the front was soon a thing of the past; France, during De Gaulle's period as minister, suffered the most comprehensive and humiliating defeat in its long history of tribulations.

Neither Paul Reynaud nor Georges Mandel, Minister of the Interior and once Clemenceau's closest colleague, nor Charles De Gaulle ever dreamed of surrendering. He and others suggested moving the seat of government to Algeria, sending all troops still capable of fighting to North Africa, and preparing a concerted attack with the English from there.

All highways were crowded with panicky refugees dashing toward the south. There were soldiers everywhere, singly and in groups, fleeing before the irresistible advance of the conquerors. The worst example was offered by French officers. More than a million soldiers surrendered—mostly without a struggle. Marshal Pétain, praised as the savior of the fatherland, was made leader of the nation. On June 17, he announced the surrender over all radio stations.

De Gaulle had flown to England twice to negotiate with British ministerial colleagues about a massive air force invasion. But everything came too late; the defeat was total. The British General Spears brought De Gaulle in a plane from Bordeaux, where Pétain and his government had settled temporarily, to London. Spears and De Gaulle left the Continent on June 17 at 9 A.M. On June 18, he made his oft-quoted speech, saying, among other things:

France is not alone. The war is not limited to the unhappy territory of our country. This war will not be
decided by the Battle of France. This war is a world war
... I, General De Gaulle, now in London, ask all
French officers and soldiers on British soil to make contact with me. Whatever may happen, the flame of
French resistance must not go out, and *will* not go out.
Tomorrow, like today, I shall speak over Radio London.

And the next day he did indeed go one step further. He
henceforth acted as a man who totally identified with *la
France* and was sure that *la France* totally identified with
him. He "took France upon himself," as he liked to put it.
He thought and still thinks: I, Charles De Gaulle, am
France, not as she is in everyday life, but as she ought to be,
in accordance with her mission and her essence. This self-assurance was first expressed on June 19, 1940: "Considering
the confusion of minds in France, the decay of a government
fallen into bondage to the enemy, I, General De Gaulle, a
soldier and leader of the French, am conscious of speaking
on behalf of France."

These words terminated the life he had led until then and
initiated him into a venture that was to throw him forever
off his charted path.

For decades he had had that mythical idea of France and
had believed in the mission he would one day carry out, but
he could never have guessed that his rise would begin with
the deepest and most humiliating fall of his nation or that
he would start his road to power at a zero point.

Retrospectively, he wrote in his memoirs:

As far as I was concerned, I began as a nullity. Neither
the shadow of any power nor that of any organization
stood at my side. I had no echo and no renown in
France, and no credit or claims abroad. But this very

lack of all means dictated my behavior. Only by making the cause of national salvation my own, totally and with no reservations, could I acquire authority. . . .

Karl Marx wrote that Louis Bonaparte, the founder and ruiner of the Second Empire, was destined to become everything because he was nothing. In 1940, Charles De Gaulle was anything but nothing. The fifty-year-old man combined outstanding qualities with unusual gifts and knowledge, a faculty of perceptiveness and insight into confused circumstances with the awareness—strengthened in misfortune—of being born for a special destiny and a special mission. Thus, when stressing in his memoirs how deprived he was of all means, how little he had and how little he was in the great play of powers, he does so to justify an excessive claim: precisely because he was so poor and powerless, he had to demand recognition, ranks, and honors with every single gesture. For he alone *was* France, a real France, whereas the other France beyond the Channel was cheering the old Marshal who had used his well-deserved fame to make defeat acceptable and honorable.

Let us now try to grasp the public effect of De Gaulle. This is no easy thing to do, and it has become increasingly difficult since 1940 because Charles De Gaulle deliberately, purposely, and at times with no effort on his part, emits the iridescent stuff of which legends are made.

One need merely have a look at De Gaulle's position in England, his relations with the Allies, especially with Roosevelt, and the special conduct which amid the worst fighting made him a center of attention for a few hours or a few days. We know that the first military actions initiated under the banner of De Gaulle's Committee met with bloody failure, at Mers El Kebir and Dakar. The subsequent battles in Syria revealed the internal contradictions of De Gaulle's policy on England. He practically forced the British to military intervention for which he didn't have adequate means, but when it was over he insisted on having it regarded as a purely French matter. Before the battle he complained that there were too few Englishmen; after the victory the English had won, there were too many of them. His chief aim was always to insist aggressively on France's sovereignty over the Allies in all her overseas territories.

Even if one observes that difficult period in the light of Gaullism and studies it with the help of De Gaulle's war memoirs, one cannot help but feel that the head of the Free French in London, although dependent on the English in every way, fought against them constantly during the years in which they had to pay for every Free French uniform and gallon of gasoline.

This is naturally an impressive proof of independence and perhaps of great character. De Gaulle has always remained loyal to the principle which he could only apply in those days thanks to Churchill's intelligent generosity. One has to know it if one cares to understand his convoluted politics. Like a spoiled child that demands everything of his parents and offers them as little as possible because he is convinced that they would never abandon him, De Gaulle is totally inconsiderate of anyone he believes to be averse to breaking with him—i.e., with France.

He considered it completely natural to demand all the more aid, consideration, and even respect the weaker he was. Yet there is no case on record in which he gave in to a similar demand on anyone else's part.

He doesn't feel obligated to any gratitude nor limited by any considerateness as long as he takes France "upon himself" or identifies with her. This man, completely beyond reproach, absolutely clean, and morally severe in his private affairs, is, when it comes to politics, a harsh and generally successful Machiavelli.

Who can doubt that De Gaulle is a very good politician? The old man has reached the zenith of his power; his prestige throughout the world is incomparable. When he runs for president, his opponents look like miniature figures. And yet I question whether he *is* a good politician.

Such skepticism on my part may suggest that I am an anti-Gaullist. Well, I'm neither an anti- nor a pro-Gaullist. I am an absolute opponent of any form of autocracy. I find it bad and unworthy of a nation to let a man, albeit as unselfish, as intellectually important, and as liberal as De Gaulle, have all power in his hands. And he has much too much power, more than any king or emperor, more than even Louis XIV or Napoleon ever had in France. This is dangerous as long as De Gaulle heads the state; afterwards, his inevitable exit will create huge and threatening problems for the country.

He does realize this himself. Perhaps that's why he warned the French nation that it would be heading for a catastrophe if it failed to re-elect him. This is a demagogical exaggeration unfortunate in every way, but De Gaulle is one of those intelligent men who believe their own exaggerations because they are enchanted by the echo of their own voices.

Naturally no one can resist the effect of a victory. History is written in the light of victories. Thus, except for his enemies, all of De Gaulle's contemporaries are convinced that the General freed and saved a France totally finished in 1940.

And now, in order to distinguish two connected and yet totally different matters, a few questions would be in order.

First of all: If De Gaulle hadn't existed, or if someone else or even no one had been in his place, would the Second World War have ended in exactly the same way? Would the

Wehrmacht have been driven out of France as it was out of Belgium and Holland? Would France have been restored as a sovereign state to its borders of 1939?

Most "if" questions are academic, a game that amuses only if it doesn't last too long, and is acceptable only if not taken seriously. But the above questions can be answered objectively. One can boldly reply "yes" to all of them: The war would have ended in exactly the same way; France, thanks to the victory of the Allies, would have regained its independence just like all the other German-occupied countries of Western Europe.

Another, more complex question: Would the *Résistance* have emerged if it hadn't been for De Gaulle and the group of Free French that he founded?

Here, too, the answer is "yes." But this doesn't bring us to the real problem. Underground movements arose in all occupied countries; each movement had a different character, a different political make-up, and different goals. The *Résistance* initially cited De Gaulle, and his appeal of June 18, only to a limited extent, and the appeal itself generally went unnoticed. Characteristically, one of the very first groups to form a policy of resistance consisted of intellectuals who were almost all anti-Stalinist leftists; their leaders were several cultural and biological anthropologists at the Musée de l'homme in Paris. They didn't need De Gaulle's appeal to be against capitulation, nor his directions to act on their own. Furthermore, like the initiators of so many other, mainly left-wing resistance groups, they were initially suspicious of De Gaulle, since they considered him a disciple of the ultra-reactionary royalist Charles Maurras.

The more active the *Résistance* became, the more it needed the help of the English, who often gave support without the mediation of the London Gaullists. The effectiveness of the movement was modest for several months, for, at least until the spring of 1941, the majority of Frenchmen sided with Pétain.

This latter position changed as Hitler's victory became more dubious and England's defeat more improbable. The *Résistance,* at first consisting of small, mostly isolated groups, now began seeking organizational unity, to expand local actions into national ones. Thus Gaullism became more and more important. Pétain's popularity remained unchallenged in all those strata that preferred to be apolitical, but even his followers were slowly yielding to the conviction that the Marshal was simply stalling for time and that at the right moment he would join with De Gaulle to free France.

When the outcome of the war became certain, a good portion of the French people were at last ready to approve of the *Résistance.* Only those who managed to furnish themselves with a praiseworthy *Résistance* past could join the victory celebration as triumphant warriors. Most Frenchmen, however, didn't dare present such claims; they had been adverse and then inactive; now in any event it was too late. And then came De Gaulle and offered them a miraculous opportunity: He declared everything that happened between 1940 and 1944, the beginning and the end of the occupation, to be legally and politically void. This legalist gamble succeeded beyond all expectation, precisely because the French had a stake in identifying with those people who turned out to be right in repudiating Pétain, in resolutely rejecting any collaboration, and in remaining loyal to the Allies. The same, peculiar psychological process that enabled Charles De Gaulle to embody France permitted countless Frenchmen to participate retroactively in De Gaulle's France-in-exile. They merely had to become Gaullists and commit themselves to the master of destiny as trustingly as they had been indifferent four years earlier to his death sentence and to the frenzied libel of him and his politics.

Thus, in 1944, and subsequently, Gaullism was the result of an identification process through which Frenchmen completely mastered an undesirable past and were assured of participation in a glorious present.

After the grave and traumatic experience that the terrible debacle of 1940 was for all Frenchmen, the *Résistance* was the start of self-therapy. The nation would probably have remained a victim of its trauma for a long time if De Gaulle had not inspired his people with the courage to rise up as a nation. No one has yet come up with a detailed account of this process between 1944 and 1946. But as certainly as the outcome of the war would have been the same even without De Gaulle, France, traumatized, would have remained at the mercy of political and moral perils if De Gaulle had not interfered and if he hadn't been the man he has remained, with all his qualities and defects.

We know that in 1944 he did not refuse the cooperation of the Communists; he even sought it in Algeria and expanded it in Paris. Yet few historians—as well as his opponents—have sufficiently pointed out in how short a time he attained the dissolution of the Communist civil-war army. In this case, as in many other areas of national life, De Gaulle quickly restored state authority solidly and cunningly. The heir to both Richelieu and the Jacobins, he recognized the validity of only the one and indivisible nation and fought against the least limitation of central authority as an attack on the vital nerve of the nation. He was and is always ready to treat as secondary and to deal tolerantly with anything that doesn't touch the sovereignty of the state. This is why he saw Stalin as the mighty Tsar of the Russian empire and regarded Bolshevist ideology as merely an irritating, rarely useful accompaniment. For many reasons he accepted the following of all people, no matter where they came from, no matter what their religion or political convictions may have been, as long as they had taken care not to serve non-French interests. When he subsequently rejected the Communists, he stigmatized them with a single word that pilloried not so much their ideology as their submission to Moscow's directives. He called them "separatists."

During and after the war he did his best to restore to the colonial peoples their feeling of forever belonging to France. He had had frequent fights with the English about the inviolability of the French Empire; his jealous distrust gave rise to his suspicion that the Anglo-Saxons were bent on robbing France of her foreign territories.

In December 1944, in Moscow, he concluded a French-Russian alliance with Stalin, which had not the slightest value. He snatched at this opportunity to prove France's independence and rank as a great power to the western Allies, but it did him no good; he was not invited to Yalta or to Potsdam. Moscow had nothing to offer him, especially no share in the Russian zone of occupation. Despite all of De Gaulle's aggressiveness toward the Anglo-Saxons and his affront to a moribund Roosevelt, France remained dependent in every respect on the western Allies, particularly on America, who aided France not because of but despite De Gaulle's provoking policies. His colonial policies ultimately led to catastrophe. He was responsible for the war in Indo-China, which brought the Fourth Republic to the edge of the abyss, and for the bloody repression of the rebellion in Constantine, which showed the Algerians the way to civil war. De Gaulle did make plans during the war, plans providing for a liberalizing of the status of colonial countries; but what he finally offered was too little and came too late.

Between 1944 and January 1946, he could have created a personal dictatorship without the slightest difficulty. Instead, he decisively contributed to making France a democratic republic once again. But it soon became clear that the restored democracy would never permit the creation and consolidation of a strong central government, without which De Gaulle felt the prosperity of the nation and the regaining of France's grandeur would be impossible. Although he adroitly managed to maneuver the Communists out of their strong civil-war position, he never succeeded in depriving the political parties of their power. Despite the compromising past that one could reproach them with, they had all risen again and won most of their voters back. And now that the nation felt purified, thanks to De Gaulle, it did not feel comfortable in the presence of this giant; it no longer considered him desirable.

When De Gaulle suddenly announced his resignation on January 20, 1946, he trusted that neither the parties nor the nation would let him go. His intention was merely what show business refers to as a "false exit"; anxiously, he waited backstage, but no one called him to return. This was certainly one of the bitterest disappointments of his life. Weeks and months passed while he waited, prepared to yield to urgent pleas. Sick of waiting, he finally made up his mind to reconquer his place on his own initiative. In 1947, he founded the R.P.F, the gathering of the French people which, rather than being a party, was to spell death to all parties. After initially promising successes, especially in local elections, this movement lost its impetus and its attraction, which had been especially strong for the petty bourgeois and the peasants and farmers.

De Gaulle was convinced that war was imminent, and he reckoned on a moment of destiny, a moment of worst danger. That moment never came, there was no war, nor was there an internal political and economic collapse in France. The Fourth Republic, so similar to the Weimar Republic, respected by few people, incessantly ridiculed by leftist and rightist extremist parties and by De Gaulle's followers, hated and ruthlessly fought, was faced with the greatest difficulties in economy and domestic politics. It had to reconstruct France and at the same time continue the costly and destructive war in Indo-China. Yet all in all, this Republic, despite its ridiculous ministerial crises, its compromising scandals, all its waverings, managed to work real wonders. It not only built France up economically—with Marshall Plan aid naturally playing a great part; it also pushed the land that had remained stagnant since World War I into the twentieth century, renovating all its production machinery and bringing it to the highest technological level. Thus, during the few years that the Fourth Republic lasted, France entered industrial society and decisively contributed to founding the Common Market.

No, France did not collapse, and World War III did not break out; so in 1953 De Gaulle put an inglorious end to the R.P.F adventure, which could easily have led to fascism. A year later he put out the first volume of his memoirs. That same year the Mendès-France government ended the war in Indo-China; a few months later the rebellion in Algeria broke out.

De Gaulle's memoirs impressed everyone—except the ultra-rightists who have been blinded by hatred for centuries. Readers saw that De Gaulle was far more significant intellectually than had been generally assumed, and were amazed to discover in him a remarkable writer on a par with the best French memoirists. At the same time, readers became aware of the extent to which the man had coalesced with the myth he always cited and the legend that had formed around him —not without his aid.

Although his presentation of gigantic events may have been astoundingly egocentric, his intelligence and his literary capabilities prevented the effect from being absurd or ridiculous. Is it laughable of him to constantly refer to himself

in his memoirs and speeches in the third person and as
"General De Gaulle," instead of saying "I"? Let us be cau-
tious and remember that this manner may not necessarily reveal arrogance but rather just the opposite: the philosophical modesty of an elderly, experienced man fully aware of
the fact that in the not too distant future everything personal shall vanish with him, that in any event it is not made
sublime by the intervention into history of that same person
—General De Gaulle. This is why he makes the apparently
bizarre distinction, the separation—to drop the mortal
frame and emphasize all the more sharply the immortality of
the historic hero. When speaking about himself in the third
person, he means the man whose actions will be remembered
independent of his personal value, to be admired or condemned.

But to return to the middle fifties. De Gaulle, no longer
expecting to be called to help, was working on his memoirs
and starting to fear the day when he would have nothing
more to write. Someone to whom he confided this anxiety
about the future advised him to make an effort toward happiness, only to be told: "But my dear man, what are you
talking about! There's no such thing as happiness."

The General—as his followers called him, as if there were
only one general—meddled in many different things. He exerted an influence, for there was no end to the stream of people coming to him for his opinion or advice, his encouragement or guidance.

He received them in his home in Colombey-les-deux-
Églises, as well as in his office in Rue Solferino, where a few
loyal followers, one of them, Georges Pompidou, a professor
of literature turned bank official, served as secretaries. Paris
knew what De Gaulle replied to one question or another, or
what mordant aphorism he coined on one occasion or another.

People continually told new anecdotes about him, and were touched by his ironic resignation. Moreover, he began revealing a peculiar trait that people hadn't really credited him with: in private conversation, if he cared to, De Gaulle could be a psychologically adroit and convincing flatterer. Almost everyone visiting him in those years was won over, for he would come away with a compliment committing him to the General more than any political ideology. Remarkably enough, De Gaulle has combined with his thoroughly genuine haughtiness a trait which seems hardly expectable in him: indefatigable cunning. He has become one of the wiliest politicians of our time; like all sharp dealers, he does not underestimate the effects of dodges and wiles.

In those years of "wandering through the desert," De Gaulle indirectly influenced French politics in a number of ways, especially in his resolute rejection of NATO and his opposition to the European policies of Robert Schuman, Jean Monnet, and their colleagues. He never took any definite position on the Algerian question. He committed himself only to warning against any use of napalm bombs; and during the Moroccan conflict he was resolute in siding with the Sultan who had been deposed by the French government.

The press conferences in which De Gaulle expressed his criticism and fears kept on going until 1955. At this point, he seemed to resign himself to the fact that the French nation, which he continued to love beyond measure in the abstract but disdain in everyday life, wished to get along without him. In January 1958, people wishing him a happy New Year were told by him that there would be no come-back.

What happened in early summer of the same year—the grotesque *putsch* of May 13, in Algeria and its perilous consequences—is still fresh in our memories. Once again, France was faced with catastrophe; she spoke the cue, which De Gaulle had grown tired of waiting for. Nevertheless, he

came, twelve years older than he cared to be, yet elastic
enough to take advantage of the complicated confusion of intrigues with such sovereign mastery that if he ever continues
his memoirs he'll be able to say he always fought with an
open visor, clearly formulating his position from the very beginning and never concealing his goals. What happened behind the scenes was important too, but there others also
acted: Soustelle, various helpers and confederates, and finally
the Gaullist officers, who were not very numerous and who
would never have dared to act if they hadn't been sure of the
General's approval—at least in the event of success.

De Gaulle was unquestionably glad to see the Fourth Republic die and happy to supply the *coup de grâce,* but no
one can claim that he was responsible for the events, intrigues or conspiracies that led to its death, or that he organized the *putsch.* He simply possessed the ability, indispensable to a military man, to profit from any opportunity.

Amid the cheers of even non-Gaullist right-wingers,
Soustelle, Debré, and General Salan called for De Gaulle, so
that this great leader might repress the Algerian Revolution
and demonstrate to all colonial nations that France, unlike
England, was determined to keep its colonial empire together. We know that De Gaulle, however, after first performing a few zigzag motions, finally went in the other direction. Four years later he not only gave the Muslims of
Algeria national political independence by treaty, but economic security as well. He thus deprived the Europeans in
that country of their hopes and ultimately their home. Moreover, within an amazingly short time, De Gaulle freed all
French foreign territories of any importance.

De Gaulle—in a blatant contradiction of the politics he
had pursued throughout the war, in flagrant breach of the
law in accordance with which he had taken over—did what
the far Left had barely dreamt of doing, hardly formulating

it and never daring to carry it out. But De Gaulle did even more.

Ever since his youth he had been committed to the Army, regarding it as the most sublime institution in France (next to the State itself); but in his fight against the military rebels in Algeria, who had helped pave his way to power, and then in his struggle against the general staff, he devalued and almost abolished the traditional army. He forced a good number of professional officers out of the army, and beyond that, he so shook the foundations of France's right wing, to which he belonged by birth and education, that its existence has become almost ghostlike. He has, however, remained true to its dream of France's grandeur.

What has he done for this grandeur? To create an institutional basis, he abolished the almost unlimited party rule of the Third and Fourth Republic and introduced a presidential government. A lot of French statesmen had long ago realized the need for such a change; e.g., Léon Blum, who in the prison of Riom had come to the conclusion that a new constitution based on the American one would help his country toward stable government.

But De Gaulle's constitution of 1958, with its subsequent amendments, is custom-made for a single man, and not for France. Consequently, this legitimately eulogized achievement, as well as government stability, is assured only as long as De Gaulle remains president. Thus his greatest achievement remains temporary. And it is almost the only one not in contradiction to his original aims and intentions.

François Mauriac, who has been Charles De Gaulle's tireless apostle for some years now, writes:

> In moments of sadness, De Gaulle may think that he has failed to attain his goal. At least I imagine that he sometimes wonders about these things and is forced to admit to himself that his expectations have been disappointed,

that he himself has been disappointed and has disappointed others. For example, Africa. His hope of a so-called Union Française, his sole chance of pitting an empire of 100 million people against the two atomic powers, has been frustrated by destiny.

And it is precisely here, where, as Mauriac writes, he has disappointed and been disappointed by destiny, it is precisely here that we observe De Gaulle's greatest historic achievement, for he has done France an immense favor by freeing her from Algeria and all her colonies.

What remains of his mission? What is he fighting for now? How is he satisfying his need to dramatically "make history"?—Well, *plus ça change, plus c'est la même chose . . .* , for once again he is fighting against allies, fighting against them alone, and once again the issue is sacrosanct sovereignty and oh so vulnerable independence.

Who is threatening him? NATO in general and the United States in particular. For years now, at least since 1959, De Gaulle has been working on France's new liberation from any military or political integration whatsoever, from all treaties which would allow organs of NATO or American military bases in France.

Why? Because he has nothing to fear in disengaging himself from his allies: he is convinced that he will lose nothing, not even possible help, if he now avoids any obligation toward NATO. If he were afraid that other allies might follow his example, he would think twice about doing what he did.

Why, then, does he choose isolation? To keep France from being involved in a Sino-American conflict, in which the Soviet Union could not remain neutral for long and in which a thermonuclear world war would be inevitable? The argument is cogent enough, but ill-founded. If such a world war did come about, no European country could retain the privilege of neutrality. But assuming that De Gaulle was striving for this unattainable neutrality, what would happen to *la grandeur?* Or has he been harboring the insane idea that Stalin had in the summer of 1939: to bide his time neutrally until all the other powers have bled themselves white and then, with intact forces, play the autocratic umpire? De Gaulle is as cunning as Stalin, but far more intelligent and far more immune to beguiling delusions.

With or without De Gaulle, with or without a pact, France remains under America's atomic protection. As long as America is non-isolationist, a French enclave at the mercy of the enemy remains inconceivable. Naturally, De Gaulle doesn't believe that his country could stand its ground for even one hour in case of a catastrophe. *La France, la France seule* is a chauvinist slogan for times of peace, but not in a crisis. On the other hand, De Gaulle is not planning any alliance with Russia or China; he doesn't fear these powers, because he doesn't really believe that they could seriously threaten Europe in his lifetime, much less in the next few years.

Then why his isolation, which is of little military consequence and highly annoying politically?

One could regard De Gaulle's present foreign policy as a continuation of his domestic policies, as one of the means by which the French are acquiring a new self-assurance and over-compensating for the humiliating collapse of 1940. Thus, this policy of splendid isolation in regard to the allies and the courting of enemies and neutrals would be the ultimate crowning of the *Résistance,* as the fifty-year-old brigadier general dreamed of it in June 1940. And the fact that France's historical continuity would be thus assured is even more crucial to De Gaulle since he dared to legally wipe out the existence of Pétain's state with a stroke of his pen. And hasn't he made a dogma of the idea that he has been the only *legitimate* guide of French destiny since 1940, continuously—i.e., also between January 1946 and June 1958? Such a claim may sound absurd, but this man, who came too late to win the victories he planned, has had to take his victories where he found them. The decolonization undertaken by the Fourth Republic would have been a capital betrayal. This selfsame liquidation on a wider scope, carried out by him and him alone, becomes a necessary, useful, and glorious act of state, which every patriotic Frenchman ought to boast about.

One may consider psychological explanations, too; they are disquieting, for De Gaulle is an autocrat. A man accustomed to yes men in all his colleagues and who takes it for granted that he may make decisions without first getting the consent of his ministers—such a man becomes incapable of dialogue and quickly loses his patience when negotiating with anyone but the most acquiescent. He becomes a soliloquizer who in the perfection of his power prefers to offer twice as much as is asked of him instead of negotiating and making concessions.

A different, additional explanation is no less disquieting: the status accompanying power probably hasn't amused De Gaulle for some years now. He is much too *désabusé,* as the French would put it, too weary of men and their vanities, including his own. What should he do with his power? He can use it for a one-sided game that will look highly dangerous and will annoy people all the more for preventing them from making any countermove that wouldn't cost them more than it would cost the challenging player.

Finally, one might surmise that De Gaulle considers the time ripe for settling old accounts of the kind one settles with one's own family, friends, allies, but not with true enemies. De Gaulle took care of all his domestic enemies, mainly, at first, with Allied help. Today, he is flattering his

potential foes, for he has nothing to hope for from his allies
that they would not offer him in a crisis, and he believes he
has nothing to fear from them but a bad mood. Which he
never fears; not infrequently, it amuses him.

France is no longer a world power; thus a French statesman can engage in world politics only from an auxiliary position. There is no way of changing this situation. But De
Gaulle for his last act could have chosen something great,
the fulfilment of his European mission. Napoleon realized
some 150 years ago that any further war in Europe could
only be an insane civil war; and since 1945 it has been obvious that Europe, but not any of the European states, could
be a world power. France's position within any united European world power would be significant enough in every way
to satisfy any national ambition. But for the moment at least,
De Gaulle's final moves are imperiling this necessary and incipient Europe.

For the sake of France's *grandeur?* Where, then, lies the
greatness of a nation? The twenty-four-year-old Charles De
Gaulle, who went to war believing in and craving glory,
might still believe that a nation's greatness could be found
in battle. Yet

> The glory of a thousand battles is gone,
> What remains of heroism? A decaying hill,
> On which weeds stand red as fire.

After two world wars, Europe thinks exactly what Confu-
cius thought when mourning a dead warrior.

And why should De Gaulle think anything different? He,
the most important intellectual, the most educated and
probably the wisest man in power today. He is the wisest because he is unable to forget the companion who remains at
his and every man's heels: death.

"Old age, what a shipwreck!" De Gaulle exclaimed once upon thinking of an old man whom the nation trusted like a good grandfather and who incessantly advised all Frenchmen to go about their work and leave the choice of goals, means, and the power of decision up to him alone. That old man, whom Charles De Gaulle, today's television star, is getting more and more to resemble, was Pétain.

"From now on, politics will be the mainspring of tragedy; politics will replace Greek fate."

Napoleon uttered these words on the eve of his victory at Austerlitz. He could not anticipate the miserable fifth act of his tragedy—nor the irresistible speed of its approach.

De Gaulle has come to realize that politics contains an element of tragedy. It may be that precisely in order to temporarily escape this tragic certitude, he is hatching complicated intrigues in foreign politics. It may do an elderly man good to think that the future of those surviving him depends on him and that they still need him urgently because he alone can undo the knots.

No head of state is attacked and caricatured as viciously in his own country as De Gaulle. This proves of course how liberal the absolute king Charles the Unique has remained. It's very easy to caricature this great man, to depict him as a Don Quixote, going to fat and incorporating Sancho Panza's opportunism and cunning. But as we know, only very young readers laugh at the tardy knight. As they grow older, they realize his tragedy and discover their own in his.

Even to non-Gaullists like myself, De Gaulle's greatness seems incontestable. It is tragic because every one of his victories has contributed to destroying the standards with which he believes he can judge and decide. It is tragicomical because he still believes in his victory and is overstaying his welcome.

Decline takes up too much time in the history of nations

and civilizations as well as in the life of individuals. Fare-
wells take too long and exits are missed. There are attempts
to hide this by confusing the setting sun with the dawn; and
grandeur is proclaimed at precisely the moment when it is
irretrievably lost for all time.

November 1965

The Mute Prophet

JOSEPH ROTH's novel *The Mute Prophet* was first published in Germany in 1966. The author actually finished
its first draft in 1927, and polished up details over the next
two years. He was never to finish, however, for on May 2,
1939, the ill-treated refugee died miserably in a Parisian
charity ward.

Born in Brody, a Jewish *shtetl* in East Galicia, on September 2, 1894, Roth was only forty-five at the time of his death.
Nevertheless, even his first writings—novellas, novels, and
nonfiction—reveal the hand of a master. He became known
at an early date—especially for his novel *Flight without End*
(*Flucht ohne Ende*), 1931—and acquired renown two years
later for *Job* (*Hiob*), which was translated into a number of
languages. This was followed in yet another two years by the
masterpiece *Radetzky March* (*Radetzkymarsch*).

During the six years of his Paris exile, Roth wrote no
fewer than six novels, plus *The Legend of the Holy Drinker*
(*Die Legende des Heiligen Trinkers*) and his polemical, malicious, and yet optimistic essays, which he brought out under
the title *The Anti-Christ.*

His newspaper work was not merely a livelihood, but a
compulsion, as he was incapable of remaining neutral on any
question. He would commit himself unrelentingly, and was

constantly fighting against something—everything interested him. He sympathized with all living creatures, especially human beings, but he had no sympathy for himself. His was the gradual suicide of an alcoholic, uncharitable treatment in the charity ward completing the process.

Several excerpts from the posthumous novel appeared in newspapers while Roth was still engaged in the writing, and readers guessed that the main character was Trotsky, for those days marked the beginning of the passion of this revolutionary—who had founded the Red Army only to be removed from office by Stalin, expelled from the Communist Party, exiled to Kirghisia, and finally banished from the Soviet Union. While Roth was working on the novel, however, the systematically total and totalitarian falsification of history had not yet reached its acme. Scarcely more than a decade before, every newspaper reader had had a day-by-day account of how Lyov Davidovich Trotsky, who apparently had ascended from deepest obscurity into bright light, was organizing a revolution and spiriting an army into existence —an army that suffered seemingly final defeats throughout the gigantic land, but survived to start winning victories itself and ultimately to annihilate the countless civil-war armies. No sooner was Lenin's name mentioned than Trotsky's followed; they were the Dioscuri of revolution, of the Russian Revolution, and of the coming World Revolution.

Trotsky was a major topic of conversation, and not only among Communists and politically interested contemporaries —his rapid rise and his inexplicable fall moved the hearts and minds of all. There was something legendary about this man, something both fascinating and repulsive. There was no dearth of authors tempted to write about him, to metamorphose him, more or less, into a fictional character, or to draw universal precepts from his life and fate in essays, or to discuss him in the terms of philosophy of history.

Joseph Roth, who had been born and raised at the border between Austria and Russia and had, moreover, fought on the Russian front in the Austro-Hungarian army during World War I, and even served as an occupation officer in the Ukraine—Joseph Roth felt he was particularly qualified to write about Russia, her Revolution, and her revolutionary heroes. He was in his mid-thirties and slowly approaching the zenith of his creative powers; and he thought he knew life, the sublime illusion of ultimate victory and the unspeakable sorrow of undeserved and senseless defeat, loneliness beyond redress, the misfortune of loving and being loved, and the dreadful misery of not loving.

Joseph Roth thought he knew what wisdom is, and he knew how useless wisdom almost always has to be; nor was he unaware that at times malevolent cunning can be equally useless. He knew all this and expressed his knowledge in a diction that brought new tones to German prose. Actually he was part of the Austrian tradition in literature, which had produced—to name just the deceased—Schnitzler and Hofmannsthal, Rilke, Trakl and Kafka, Karl Kraus and Robert Musil. But he was the youngest, born too late, far too late. The old empire had crumbled to dust by the time he, a veteran of World War I, began writing.

During the rise of the Nazis and after his escape from Hitler's Germany, Joseph Roth was overcome by a positively juvenile homesickness for the lost empire; he became a monarchist and devoted all his energy to the pitiful propaganda disseminated by Austrian émigrés for the benefit of Otto von Habsburg. Roth's novel *Radetzky March,* published late in 1932, was his singular monument to old Austria. There is hardly a work in modern literature that expresses the nostalgia for an irretrievable past with such *doloroso* irony, such tender melancholy, and yet with such wise and conciliatory love.

When Roth started working on his so-called Trotsky novel—only five years earlier—he had felt anything but Austrian. Having lived in Germany for seven years, he considered himself a German and sincerely desired to be one. This is startling but not incomprehensible, for since his childhood Roth had been grappling with the problem of his identity. The problem was insoluble because he himself re-created it every day.

In his autobiographical writings the Galician Jew often presented himself as the half-Jewish son of a Russian Jewess and an Austrian Catholic; most of the time he passed himself off as the child of a vagabond, who had deserted his family and, without ever sending word of his whereabouts, had died in an Amsterdam insane asylum. Roth claimed that he himself had been born in Schwabendorf (a small German colony near his real hometown, Brody). His identity alternated between Jewish and Catholic, Russian, German, and Austrian, and he falsified his biography with curious humbug in other ways as well. Joseph Roth most certainly did know his father, who was no Catholic but a Jew from Brody, probably an enthusiastic follower of the Chassidic mystics; he died relatively young, of tuberculosis. Relatives in Vienna took charge of young Joseph and made it possible for him to go to school.

"The life story of Kargan [the protagonist of *The Mute Prophet*] has no more of a topical tendency than any other story. It is not an illustrative model of a political viewpoint —at most, it is illustrative of the ancient and enduring truth that the individual is always vanquished."

Who would care to argue with the writer as to how incontestable and how timeless this truth really is? Everyone knows the individual is always vanquished. But it is equally true that the defeat of most people is, at the same time, a transition to the succeeding generations. An individual is immortal so long as there is someone alive who retains some memory of him.

Just who was this Friedrich Kargan, who, though not identical with Trotsky, is still the central character of the so-called Trotsky novel, and whose destiny is the same as the politician's? This is how Kargan's life begins:

> Friedrich was born in Odessa, in the home of his grand-father, the wealthy tea-dealer Kargan. The child, un-wanted because he was illegitimate, was the son of an Austrian piano teacher named Zimmer, whom the wealthy tea-dealer had not permitted to marry his daughter. The piano teacher left Russia; old Kargan, learning that his daughter was pregnant, instituted a search for the piano teacher, but to no avail. —Half a year later, Kargan sent her and the baby to his brother, a well-to-do businessman in Trieste. Friedrich grew up in his uncle's home. His childhood was not totally un-happy despite his falling into the hands of a benefactor.

Except for being born in the Ukraine, the hero has little in common with Trotsky. Instead, Kargan represents a re-current type in Joseph Roth's works: this type is always threatened by the uncertainty of his origins, uneasy over his lack of a father, and dependent on relatives in whose home the lonely child is raised. Although the mother does not run off as the father does, she nevertheless remains completely in the background and soon drops out of sight.

Young Friedrich Kargan becomes a clerk in a travel agency, which eventually sends him to a town on the Austri-an-Russian border—a town to which the plot of almost every Roth novel will lead at some point. Here Kargan works with specialists in human contraband, smugglers who guide deserters, Jewish emigrants, and other refugees from Russia across the border to a port from which they are usually shipped to America.

In the course of one of these nocturnal adventures, Kargan meets an imposing man, the Russian revolutionary Savelli. Subsequently, in Vienna, Savelli introduces him to various fellow revolutionaries, who are indicated only by the initials of their last names: R. (Radek), L. (Lenin), and others. Kargan joins the revolutionaries, goes to Russia for them illegally, is arrested and deported to Siberia, escapes just at the beginning of World War I, flees westward, reaches Austria, and eventually arrives in Switzerland, where Lenin has set up headquarters. Later, together with Lenin and his comrades, he returns to Russia to spur the incipient revolution. Kargan becomes the great orator and commander, the unique propagandist and the leading strategist of the civil war. Then, however, Savelli, to whom the author lends Stalin's features, discharges Kargan, sends him off to a diplomatic post abroad, orders him back, and deports him and his closest comrades-in-arms to Siberia.

Kargan's reasons for becoming a revolutionary are explained several times, but not convincingly. One cause of this peculiar gap may reside in Roth's having worked on the novel intermittently; he would frequently stop writing and then return to it in a different mood. Two or three versions of the manuscript exist, and it is only thanks to Werner Lengling's laudable editorial labor that the novel could assume its present, definitive form.

Beyond the foregoing explanation—an insufficient though not insignificant one—there may be a deeper reason, and the only crucial one at that. Joseph Roth was possessed by his basic themes as by an unrecognized compulsion. Whatever raw material, subject matter, plot, era, milieu, he might have chosen, he always yielded to an inner compul-

sion to draw the typical Roth protagonist: a rootless, direc-
tionless man, always at odds with himself yet always acting
with utmost decision, and thereby evolving into a hero able
at times to believe in himself.

Kargan tells the Russian revolutionary R., whose irony
and skeptical common sense fascinate him, "I'm a poor man
on the side of the poor. The world is not good to me, and I
don't want to be good to the world. Its injustice is enormous. I suffer from its injustice. Arbitrary power hurts me. I
want to hurt the powerful."

Now this explanation might make sense if we could believe that Kargan really is poor; but he's not. To recall the
parallel to Trotsky: like all intellectual revolutionaries in
Russia—almost without exception—Trotsky came from a
well-to-do home. As far as I know, none of them was afflicted
by poverty: Rosa Luxemburg grew up in very good material
circumstances, in a relatively wealthy Jewish family which
she left in order to devote herself to the revolution; she put
up lightheartedly with continual destitution as one of the
consequences. The same holds for Angelica Balabanova (who
died recently at an advanced age), and for Bukharin, Rakov-
sky, and even for Lenin himself.

Elsewhere, Kargan says, "You don't just come defenseless,
homeless, and as an outlaw into a hostile world and then let
the world take its course. You're not given intelligence in
order to put it in the service of stupidity; you don't just have
eyes in order to lead the blind." These are the key words:
homeless—outlaw—hostile world.

Joseph Roth's *Mute Prophet* is very eloquent in express-
ing his skepticism about the world and the meaning of life;
he had a heterodox attitude toward any revolutionary refor-
mation, any utopian belief in the future. The strangest thing
about his book is a badly disguised, barely comprehensible
contradiction: Kargan is portrayed as a model revolutionary,

as an exemplary soldier and commander who becomes world-famous for his exceptional victories. Yet, at the same time, the writer never stops proving that Kargan doesn't believe in anything, cannot believe in anything, that he is incapable of genuine enthusiasm. Apart from the above-quoted utterances Kargan never comes out with anything revealing social consciousness, and yet a revolutionary lacking this is inconceivable, psychologically, philosophically, or politically.

Kargan writes in his journal, "We are meant to prepare a revolution but probably not to witness the happy outcome of a victorious one. I am as incapable as R. of believing that any changes are possible in the world: except for changes of nomenclature." Kargan sets down these words just a few years before the revolution that will place him and those like him at the center of world-shaking events. No complicated evidence is needed to prove that no revolutionary ever thought, spoke, or wrote in this manner—at least not before his action was completed, before the "post-victory hangover." In the thousands of pages written by Marx and Engels, Liebknecht and Rosa Luxemburg, Lenin, Trotsky, and Bukharin, no reader will ever come across such nihilism, able to justify inactivity, indolent cynicism, or individual careerism. Naturally a person who had broken with the Revolution and achieved some distance from it could echo Kargan's words. Yet Kargan writes them in his journal while still a young revolutionary activist whose exceptional fate is as yet unknown. Later, after being "disengaged" and sent abroad, he tries to come to terms with what has happened; but he merely repeats his previous statements. " 'I serve without any faith,' Friedrich said to himself. 'Twenty years ago, I would have been called a scoundrel. I get a salary, yet I have no conviction. I despise the people I associate with, I don't believe this revolution will succeed.' "

Kargan is already the prophet gone mute, unconsciously

hoping for banishment and dreaming of a *Flight without End*—as do most of Joseph Roth's heroes.

So much for Kargan; we realize that he is no Trotsky, that he has virtually nothing in common with the exile who led the October Revolution only to be vilified beyond measure and assassinated by Stalin. Kargan is no Trotsky, whatever the author's original intention may have been when, deeply impressed by Trotsky's life and fate, he began to write this novel.

But what sort of person is Kargan, whom the author constantly involves in revolutionary activity? What is he if not a revolutionary? If anything, he is a neurotic rebel; and thus, no matter what he does, he is essentially the very opposite of a revolutionary.

The frequent failures in literary depictions of revolutionaries almost always involve the same error: The author seeks a purely individual, psychological basis for his hero's decision to join the revolution. In Kargan's case it is the complex homelessness, Roth's characteristic lack of identity. In the case of young Hugo in Sartre's political drama *Dirty Hands (Les Mains sales)*, it is a tension that can be explained psychoanalytically as Hugo's purely psychogenic conflict with his father and his bourgeois background. Both cases, and many others, betray a fundamental misconception in other areas. One example: An extreme neurotic hypersensitivity may be uncommonly beneficial, and at times even indispensable, to artistic creation. Yet a man becomes an artist, not because he is neurotically hypersensitive, but in spite of it, through a creative counter-process. The neurotic makes himself the object of his hypersensitivity, whereas the artist uses his hypersensitivity and everything connected with it to create his work.

A neurotic reaction against poverty, against oppressive paternal authority or the absence of a father, against tyrannical pampering or humiliating neglect, against an envied brother, cousin, and so forth—any of these, under certain personal, family, and social conditions, may force a person to seek salvation in rebellion. This rebellion can manifest itself in a variety of actions, including the criminal, sexual, and political. A rebel can just as easily join a revolutionary movement as a counterrevolutionary one. He can parrot any dictum of social consciousness, yet the awareness itself remains alien to him. Mutiny, insurrection, rebellion, revolution are merely fluke opportunities that he takes advantage of. Rather than serving an idea or a movement, he does the opposite: he tries to exploit a great cause to find escape from his own existence—that is, to rid himself of unbearable obligations so that he may become a hammer instead of the anvil he feared he would always be.

Sartre's Hugo could have become a drug addict instead of casting his lot with the revolutionary movement; and the murder he finally commits—whatever Sartre intended—is in no wise a political act.

We all know the gaudy historical novels in which wars and revolutions, earthquakes and every conceivable kind of calamity combine to create a flame-lit backdrop, a gigantic stage-setting for the usual sentimental adventures. We need only imagine for a moment that these sets are gone to discover that the events are not historical and the destinies not universal; all we are left with is eternally harassed innocence, secret love affairs, evil villains, and virtuous rescuers. The fact that you can light a cigarette on an apocalyptic conflagration does not mean that a burning match can substitute for the apocalypse.

In Joseph Roth, in Sartre, and in quite a number of other equally distinguished writers, the failure to depict a true revolutionary can be traced back to several causes, the consistent and decisive one possibly being that there are certain situations and experiences that a writer can easily picture and yet not successfully portray if he hasn't experienced them himself. I am thinking primarily of three vital situations and the concomitant experiences. First of all, you have to be a father or a mother to grasp the relationship between parents and their child, a relationship that is speciously simple and yet transforms the entire life of a human being. The second situation is that of a prisoner. An acute reader will easily discover whether a writer has personally undergone imprisonment or relies merely on other people's experiences and stories for his treatment of the theme. The third situation is that of the revolutionary, and particularly when he is an intellectual. Here I would like to add a comment deserving of reflection:

The most convincing portrayals of the experience of revolution are to be found in authors who in some manner, but always tragically, have broken with the revolution. Joseph Roth, thanks to an unusual writing talent, can express ideas and perceptions which he can yet do little to actualize in his novels—precisely because, though possibly a rebel for a while, he was never a revolutionary. Consequently I was deeply impressed at reading, "The great happiness of having suffered at some point for a magnificent idea and for humanity has crucial bearing on our decisions long after skepticism has opened our eyes, made us realize the truth, and deprived us of hope. We have walked through fire and are branded for the rest of our lives."

This is a profound truth, in the light of which any number of books characteristic of our era have been written—by Victor Serge, Ignazio Silone, Malraux, Koestler, and others.

In another passage Roth grazes a basic realization of the essence of a revolutionary. His protagonist says, "My conviction has become a passion because I'm what your vocabulary would call 'homeless.' I'm going to war for a world in which I can be at home."

The rebel usually acts under the compulsion of a generally negative passion perpetuated by his feeling of having been wronged, by immense megalomania, and by a tormenting inferiority complex. Under certain circumstances it may appear that such passion can produce conviction. *Weltanschauung* or zealotism, political commitment, ideological fanaticism—in such cases these things are not the modalities so much as the variable expressions of emotion that only seems socially oriented but in reality is invariably egocentric: a boundless selfishness.

The revolutionary, on the other hand, can be characterized by the fact that his "conviction becomes a passion."

Precisely because, at bottom, Roth delineates merely a rebel, he leaves out all the concrete elements that might have made the revolutionary movement and its political and moral degeneration comprehensible and intelligible. In *The Mute Prophet* all this is reduced to an extremely vague and far too fleeting shadow play. We don't really know what the fight was about and we never find out why the revolutionaries, who were the closest of friends before their victory, are driven apart and eventually turn into the worst of enemies.

The Mute Prophet is a very fine book; there are marvelous passages in it—descriptions of landscapes and moods, analyses of emotions, hesitant feelings, passionate surges. There are model formulations of wise perception, meaningful truths, and revealing observations. Thus we can love this novel even while we reject the author's claim to writing the tragedy of a revolutionary.

Joseph Roth always manages greatly to transcend himself: to understand relations he hasn't known, to divine facts he actually meant to refute. This is proof of the abundance of miracle in all true literature.

Djilas, or Repentance Punished

~~~~~~

IN astonished silence we hear the sighs of a penitent man who proclaims the folly of his sins. We are not displeased when a man lays bare his past and, to escape it, inflicts upon himself as much pain as he would on the most loathsome of enemies. Nevertheless, it will not do for the monologue of the lonesome penitent to last too long. Even the remorseful man must obey the law of good taste, which ordains that the penitent not accuse himself before the beginning of the last act. The final scene belongs to the survivors clustering forgivingly around the grave of the repentant sinner.

The contrite man, like the hero after his triumph, must vanish very quickly, must not become an encumbrance to even the most generous of his contemporaries. This applies particularly to a man who has lost power and then indulges in such self-accusation as openly to condemn both power and the rulers who are disposed to continue their rule and enjoy their privileges. The crown prince who renounces the throne and makes himself a beggar or the prophet of a new faith should be careful not to pass judgment on the king or the courtiers' mores if he does not wish to attract universal hostility.

Of all Communists who have voluntarily broken with their party, Milovan Djilas has been the only one who, faced with a final choice, decided to give up his position. He dissociated himself from the leaders who have governed Yugoslavia since 1945. Since January 1954 he has been waging an unequal struggle all by himself, and the outcome does not seem uncertain. And yet. . . .

The conflict in the Djilas case goes far beyond him and his writings, his past errors and his present sufferings. And it concerns a great deal more than simply Tito, his regime, and Yugoslavia. Yet it primarily involves a man who, since his rupture with power, has been sequestered in the most disheartening solitude: that of a man persecuted by people he quite recently still loved and felt himself loved by, both in despair and on the crest of victory—the twofold solitude of a prisoner who cannot forget that his guards are his brothers-in-arms and who knows that his fellow prisoners will never forget that once he was the most ruthless of their enemies.

Milovan Djilas was born in 1911, in the late hours of a capricious day in spring, as he explains in his autobiography *Land without Justice*. His mother had to keep the birth a secret, since it was regarded as shameful to bear a child before the family house was completely ready. The Djilases had settled in Podbisce near Kolasin, where the father had been promoted to command of the border guard.

The topography of this province includes both battlefields and areas of extermination. Montenegrins, forced by the Turks to convert to Islam, had been decimated here—killed in their fields, forests, in meadows under the fierce sun; the survivors had fled. Christians, triumphant fratricides, inherited their huts and their villages.

Djilas is the son of a people who never could learn to rest, always refused to acknowledge defeat, and for more than five hundred years—since June 28, 1389—had never stopped fighting a cruel guerrilla war against the Turks.

In this land, the children were taught only one fear: that of showing fear. And so they always practiced the courage that drives a man to seek danger, or evoke it through fool-hardiness. Djilas remained faithful to this courage even later —as an illegal activist and as functionary of the Communist Party.

In the 340 pages of his autobiography, Djilas waxes poetic whenever his love for his native soil frees him from himself, releasing him from the solitude he has been living in ever since his break with communism. The gloomy mountains, the stony soil, the poor villages of his tiny homeland are cherished in his memory. And he discloses his friendship with his older brother Aleksa:

> Nothing could separate us, everything bound us to-gether. Without the love I felt for him, I would hardly have known what real love is, which nothing can de-stroy or submerge in oblivion. His death before a firing squad may have been easier if he had time to think of my love.

Djilas was three years old by the outbreak of World War I, which drained Serbia far more than other nations. Monte-negro, occupied by the Austrians in 1916, was exposed to famine, epidemic, and—more violently than ever—internal discord. Little Milovan early made the acquaintance of violence—the violence that defies and degrades before it re-presses, that kills unhesitatingly. Before leaving Berane, the town in which he attended *Gymnasium,* Milovan already considered himself a Communist. He accepted the theory of violence in communism as readily as he was attracted by its apocalyptic threats. The *coup d'état* of January 6, 1929, through which the king set up his dictatorship, increased the conviction of Djilas and so many like him that all conditions had to be changed and the state revolutionized fundamentally.

In Belgrade, Djilas registered in the University's philosophical faculty and immediately began to take part in various student actions organized (or at least inspired) by the illegal Communist Party. In 1932 he became an active member of the Party; he soon attracted attention and was quickly given important tasks. A year later he was arrested and sentenced to three years' imprisonment in Sremska Mitrovica, whose prison became a kind of political university that trained the middle-level and higher functionaries of the Party.

In 1936, just released, Djilas resumed his political activity, which had the strange underground character both caused and made possible by Balkan and South American dictatorships; in which waves of brutal persecution alternated with a tacit tolerance of the illegals. Amazing moderation by the regime, which seems to announce a restoration of all freedoms, is followed by even greater repression.

Milovan Djilas was well known in the intellectual circles of Belgrade and Zagreb. Even the police were not unaware of his part in the underground movement. This did not prevent Josip Broz-Tito from giving him increasingly important assignments in the newly formed leadership of the Party. The Stalinist liquidation, which gradually wiped out all the leaders of the Yugoslav Party in Moscow, accelerated Tito's rise to power and smoothed the way for the young men who were part of his close following.

After his first meeting with Tito—in Zagreb in 1937—Djilas' career took a new turn. He climbed higher and higher, until his break with the party hurled him into the abyss. As a member of the Central Committee, he took rigor-

ous measures against any "ideological deviation," in which
he sensed objective if not subjective treason. How exemplary
a Stalinist he was is demonstrated in these lines published in
October 1942, in the midst of the misery of partisan warfare:

> Is there any greater honor or deeper joy than knowing
> that Stalin is your closest comrade, the most cherished
> comrade? . . . Stalin in his constitution has realized the
> glorious poem of freedom and brotherhood between
> men and nations. Stalin is the only statesman with a
> quiet conscience and an altruistic heart . . . Stalin is the
> most perfect of men. . . . He knows everything, he sees
> everything; everything human concerns him intimately.
> . . . There are no enigmas that Stalin cannot solve and
> no secret that he cannot reveal. . . .

Djilas was always the zealous functionary of Stalinism in
word and deed, his doubts always turning into distrust, followed by a penal decree. Vladimir Dedijer, in his autobiography *The Beloved Land,* tells how his friend Djilas ordered
him not to help the young poet Oscar Davičo, who in 1938
had just finished a five-year prison sentence. The very fact
that this young writer had suffered so greatly for the Communist cause made his daring to write like a Surrealist all
the more intolerable. He had to be unmasked for the "Trot-
skyite" he was; sympathizers—Dedijer among them—had to
be prevented from assisting the poet in his misery. "Davičo
is primarily a Surrealist," Djilas declared. "Don't you realize
that the Party makes men but is also fully capable of destroying them the moment they depart from the Party line?"

It was Djilas who waged the struggle against the Communists and sympathetic intellectuals who had rallied around
the great writer Miroslav Krleža and his magazine; all
thought they could reject obscurantism and still remain true
to the cause. The hunt for "deviators" nevertheless persisted
and continued indefatigably, even when Hitler's threats

were becoming more and more dangerous, Fascism was pro-
ceeding to stormy attack, and the Spanish Civil War broke
out.

But even in 1935, when the Seventh World Congress of
the Comintern resolved to discontinue the mad "class-ver-
sus-class" policy and the fight against the so-called Social Fascists, the Yugoslav Communists did not abandon their isolation and develop a popular front. The leadership refused to
give up its sectarian dogmatism and free itself of its inflamma-
tory Byzantinism.

Djilas, the guardian of ideological purity, constantly
evoked conflicts, tore down, accused, and condemned all
those who insisted on having independent opinions even in
their own fields. Krleža obstinately went on writing his novels, plays, and essays exactly as he wished. He refused to submit to Djilas, who had published only a few bad writings
and wanted to force an aesthetic line on him in the interests
of the emancipation of the world proletariat.

Without Tito's and Pijade's consent, the young bureau-
crat would never have dared to challenge such important
men constantly. But the two senior leaders felt that the
Party could not permit even a spark of skepticism, so they allowed the silencing of an intellectual who had gone so far as
to criticize Lenin's *Materialism and Empirocriticism* and Engels' *Dialectics of Nature*. No skepticism was harmless at the
time of the Moscow Trials, which also helped prepare for
Stalin's pact with Hitler.

The activities of the Yugoslav Party went on in almost
complete obscurity because of the long period of illegality.
In the verbose disputes published in temporarily legal periodicals, writers denounced one another to the Hegelian
world-spirit, the shades of Marx, Engels, and Lenin, and—

without meaning to—to the political police of the hated dictatorship.

Outside the Soviet Union, Stalinists submitted voluntarily to the shalt's and shalt-not's of the NKVD. They read nothing that contradicted the general line or that failed to praise the paradisaic perfection of the Stalinist realm and proclaim the infallibility of the father of the nations. Djilas thus never felt the slightest need to read anything but *Imprekorr* (*International Press Conference*), the weekly of the Comintern, which was smuggled along dangerous routes into Yugoslavia so that the Party activists might always know and remain true to policies. Here the bureaucrats always learned the ever-changing but always definitive answers to all political, social, and economic questions as well as the solutions to philosophic and aesthetic problems.

The German-Russian pact was an ideological acid test for every Communist and sympathizer. Anyone who wanted to enjoy the confidence of the Party apparatus had not only to approve of this change but actually to hail it as the triumph of the just cause. Tito, Djilas, and their colleagues brutally got rid of all comrades they suspected of not agreeing with the pact and the partition of Poland. Many skeptics among the Partisans were reportedly handed over to the police or even liquidated as soon as they were detected.

On July 4, 1941, the Communist Party of Yugoslavia proclaimed the necessity of a popular rebellion against the enemy occupation. In this document Tito particularly stressed that it was Yugoslavia's duty to hurry to the aid of the Soviet Union so that "heroic nation would not be alone in shedding its precious blood." Some six months after the German aerial attack on Belgrade, Tito, Djilas, Ranković, Kardelj, and their followers commenced hostilities against the Germans and the Italians, then against Ustashi and the

Serbian Fascists, and finally, after negotiations with Michai-lovič were broken off, against the Chetniki, who had been the first to rise up against the German occupation.

Since the beginning of the nineteenth century, the nations that make up present-day Yugoslavia had rebelled against foreign rule no less than twenty-eight times. Now, in late summer of 1941, without any ideology or program, they began a new fight against terrible enemies, who daily grew increasingly hateful to the resigned and more and more in-tolerable even to the most pacifistic. A *maquis* formed: in the woods, smaller and larger groups gathered, streaming to-gether on the naked mountains and on Adriatic islands. Ev-erywhere they opposed the enemy, who seemed as uncon-querable as death. They suffered defeat after defeat. Their native soil grew harder and harder to their feet. They en-dured hunger, cold, and a shortage of everything, including weapons and medical supplies for their wounded, whom they refused to abandon even when taking them along be-came a superhuman task.

The Yugoslavs were exemplary in their unfailing courage, their unlimited perseverance, their endless loyalty and pa-tience. And Milovan Djilas was one of the men who led them through all these perils. He never once hesitated to ex-pose himself to danger and always demonstrated that Monte-negran bravery which—often uselessly—emphasizes the puerility of military heroism.

Almost all the Party bureaucrats proved their mettle in the face of the enemy and thus gained a sense of confidence that their faith in the Stalinist orthodoxy merely strength-ened. This feeling (oh, dialectics!) would one day psycholog-ically ease the opposition they had to develop toward Stalin after 1948.

When the Communist Party extended its complete and to-talitarian rule over all Yugoslavia, this seemed to be the only possible solution to the problem. The Ustashi had massacred the Serbians in Croatia, Bosnia, and Herzegovina; the Chetniki had persecuted the Croats wherever they found them. Only the Communist-led army of liberation had actually abided by the principle of equality and fraternity for all Yugoslav tribes. Now, after the war, new outbursts of national hatred were feared; many people resigned themselves to living under a Communist rule in the hope that dictatorship would put an end to friction among the Yugoslav peoples and bring about a federative solution to the problem of nationalities.

Naturally, after such a war, after the rule of an Ante Pavelič, the desire for revenge drove people to murderous vendetta. Ranković and Djilas spread a reign of terror in accordance with a police concept of history, which—zealous Stalinists that they were—they applied with utmost determination. During this time, Milovan Djilas had the power autocratically to settle all earlier ideological conflicts without encountering any resistance. The books that struck him the wrong way would not strike anyone else's fancy, for they either failed to appear or vanished without a trace—as did plays, paintings, and other art that failed to win Djilas' good will.

Belgrade became a second Moscow for the postwar Communists. Marshal Tito's fame was second only to that of Generalissimo Stalin, who incidentally became jealous. Russia installed the Cominform in the Yugoslav capital and with it headquarters of those well-known organizations of good will that serve Stalinism behind their false fronts.

In Moscow, Djilas often met the man he had described as "the perfect human being." If he was disappointed, he gave no indication. Stalin, rather curious about the Montenegrin, invited him to a Caucasian spa to convalesce, and also to give the Georgian secret services the opportunity of thoroughly observing this man, who strangely enough had never realized how advantageous it can be to hold one's tongue when everyone else is shooting off his mouth.

Vladimir Dedijer, who in his book on Tito describes all phases of the schism crisis, is rather discreet when it comes to telling how his friend Djilas reacted during those weeks when the Yugoslav Communists feared losing the very ground under their feet. For, whatever they did to convince Stalin of their unlimited devotion and love, they were given a scornful brush-off. At the Fifth Congress of the Yugoslav Party, which had been excluded from the Cominform for a month, Tito ended his concluding speech with the call: "Long live the Soviet Union, long live Stalin." And the eyes of the 2344 delegates turned once again to the bust standing between the portraits of Marx and Engels, the bust of the "greatest leader of all times."

"I'll just move my little finger and—bang!—there won't by any more Tito. He'll fall!" Stalin said to his loyal Khrushchev, who in turn reported it to the Twentieth Congress of the Communist Party of the Soviet Union, adding: "Stalin moved not only his little finger but everything he was able to move; yet Tito did not fall."

He did not fall because he had at his disposal the apparatus of an authoritarian state and a secret police (molded in the image of the NKVD) that always detected in time all those who, under Stalin's direct orders, initiated the action designed to force Tito to confess that he had always been an informer for the Zagreb police and the Gestapo, an American spy, and so on. The action failed because, for the first time, Stalin attacked Communists, who were determined and able to use his methods to defend themselves against him. Stalin was thus forced not just to cry treason against a few men but to banish a whole party—a party possessing state power—and thereby an entire land, a Socialist country that had been lauded and praised by all toadies of world communism.

A year later Stalin ordered the Rajk trial, in order to compromise Yugoslavia's leaders and "unmask" the Fascist character of their dictators. Only then did Tito and his friends break with Stalin. Until the Budapest pseudo-trial, they, like all Communists, had been spreading the delirious slander so highly dramatized in the Stalinist trials, that the defendants would warp their past beyond all recognition and degrade themselves totally until a shot in the back of the neck put an end to their lives.

After the trial against Rajk, the Titoists admitted that as early as 1936—not just in 1949—Stalin had forced veteran Communists to confess in order to let them atone for crimes that had never been committed. His victims included almost all the men who had founded Yugoslavia's Communist Party and directed it until 1937.

In 1949 the Titoists renounced that part of their past in which they had pledged allegiance to an unconditional solidarity with Stalin's crimes. But they still preferred to proceed slowly and withdraw cautiously rather than draw nearer to the Social Democrats or the Trotskyites, or those true heretics among the early Communists who rejected not only Stalin's regime but also the Leninism it claimed to be based on.

We now know that Djilas felt personally threatened by Stalin's letters and all the slanderous things the Cominform spread abroad after the rupture. Two years later, in autumn of 1950, Djilas published a series of articles that in 1948 he would have condemned as an act of the basest treason. These articles disclosed to the readers of *Borba,* the Central Organ of the Party, that the Soviet Union is far from being the land

of socialism and is actually a dictatorship of a set of bureaucrats who, falsely evoking Leninism, have introduced state
capitalism and set up their own unlimited power.

It was probably that autumn that the forty-year-old, without fully realizing it, started out on the road that was irrevocably to separate him from his conformist convictions as
well as from his youth and the Party that had become his
home when he left Montenegro twenty years before.

When Djilas investigates social reality for the first time
without subjecting it beforehand to an ideological distortion, he is initially blinded by a powerful searchlight burst-
ing through darkness. He discovers the truth and realizes
that it has no resemblance whatsoever to the lie he had been
spreading with the violence of autocratic intolerance.

Like the frequently quoted *Logic of Struggle,* the disclosure of a long-rejected truth involves unexpected complications. Truth becomes a personal destiny, as Dostoievsky realized and revealed in *The Dream of a Ridiculous Man,* in
which he speaks of how difficult it is to keep a newly discovered truth to oneself and how impossible it is to refrain from
repeating it to the people one has gone astray with. By publishing his series *Topical Themes,* Djilas became a traitor in
the eyes of all Communists outside Yugoslavia. He nevertheless remained true to the Party line; he was, after all, a
leader of the Party, the most respected after Tito, who occupied a higher position than his boyhood friends Ranković
and Kardelj. Thus he was not the heretic—his Party was
heretical in its relationship to the Soviet Union.

Djilas began to study political and theoretical writings he
had hitherto condemned without bothering to read. He was
confronted with a moving experience we have all had in our
youth: books revealed to us that ideas we have looked upon

as our very own have been expressed long before us by other people. Strange voices were suddenly close to us and touched us as if we were hearing the first echoes of our own voice; sometimes it almost seemed as if those voices were coming from within us.

A member of the Politbureau, President of Parliament, Chief of Propaganda and thus ruler of the entire intellectual life of his country, Djilas discovered that he still had a great deal to learn before getting to the heart of things. He read such banned authors as Karl Kautsky, Rosa Luxemburg, and others such as the theoreticians of Democratic Socialism. "All our ideas, especially our political, economic, and social thoughts, have been shaken, and shall be shaken even more thoroughly," he writes in his article "League or Party?" in January 1954, after proclaiming on December 24, 1953, that his goal "is to abandon the unreal and abstract world of the elite and finally enter the real world: the world of simple working people and normal human relations."

Admittedly it was very late after the "Midnight of the Century" of which Victor Serge spoke when he tried to warn those who had lost their way. Jugashvili was already dead, and the dead man's most loyal comrades-in-arms were hastening to alter their past: they retrospectively studded it with gestures if not actions of protest and resistance against the vanished tyrant.

Titoism stopped being a fascism; apparently no one even cared to accuse it of so-called revisionism. All camps were opened to the Titoists, Socialism as well as peace. Somewhat later, Khrushchev himself came to Belgrade to clear up the "misunderstanding."

In point of fact, the Communist Party of Yugoslavia had never been and still is not heterodox. The rupture of 1948 was forced upon it as a result of the conflict between two ap-

paratuses of power in which the smaller one, Yugoslavia, resisted one of the countless orders of the larger one, Russia—
the order to commit suicide.

In 1948 as in 1953, in 1956 as today, the ideology of
Yugoslavia's leaders remains the same: an ideology of *false
identities*. The Yugoslav dictatorship is not that of her
Party, even less that of the proletariat or the people; what it
really is is a fundamentally bureaucratic oligarchy unwilling
to give up even the tiniest particle of its political power and
therefore unwilling to permit the emergence of even the
slightest political group that might strive for any sort of independence. On the other hand, the Titoist regime *has*
made significant economic concessions. It has thus returned
the soil to the peasants and allowed the workers' councils to
play a major part in the management of factories. Last but
not least, Tito's regime has restored quite a number of liberties. Citizens, particularly non-Communists, may express dis-
senting opinions about philosophical, aesthetic, and economic questions. Nevertheless, the leaders do remain alert,
their suspicions aroused by any divergence among members
of the bureaucracy itself, an attitude that recalls the distrust
by Prussian kings of their officers.

Power actually belongs to a *new ruling class*. This is the
conclusion Milovan Djilas finally reached—after so many
others who said and proved the very same thing before him.
But these men did not belong to his class and had no share
of its power. Djilas, however, as it were, attacked himself; he
leveled accusations at his own power. He excluded himself
from this new class, banning himself to the no-man's land
that is the homeland of rebels without any party or support.

What a curious adventure! He had set out in search of
propagandistic arguments to defend Tito and his regime
against Stalin's campaign of political annihilation. En route
he encountered the truth about the proletarian dictatorship

in the Soviet Union. That was how he discovered what this dictatorship meant in his own land. In his mirror, he saw a man he had to fight against, as well as his friend Tito and all his comrades-in-arms.

The final episode before the breach starts with the article "The New Contents," published in *Borba* on October 11, 1953, and ends with the article "Revolution," which appeared on January 7, 1954. In between, Djilas produced fifteen other articles that, although written in the usual Party jargon, questioned all the convictions of members of the Communist group. The Communists were momentarily at a loss, but they easily hastened to conform to the new Party line just as they had always done in the past to the old. Naturally they believed that what Djilas wrote was "official." They were already swearing that they were entirely convinced. But they were soon to realize that they had made a mistake, and they speedily did an about-face.

On December 26, 1953, the Parliament unanimously made Djilas president. Four weeks later, this same Djilas was removed from office. Now he was nothing, not even an unimportant delegate: Titograd, the new capital of Montenegro, which had sent him to the Skupština with a majority vote of 98.8 per cent, demanded the immediate annulment of his mandate in the name of 100 per cent of the voters.

Those good people were in a terrible hurry to put themselves at a visible distance from Djilas, for suddenly he was finished; after all, the Central Committee had thrown him out at its session of January 17, 1954. And Djilas showed himself in a strange light; one might almost have thought him mentally deranged, for example, when he almost humbly asked for the right to take part in the vote against himself. Only two of his friends and followers were still willing to defend him: Mitra Mitrovica, his former wife, and Dedijer, who defended him with eloquence and courage. Djilas was opposed by Tito—who, with more pity than violence, reproached him not so much for his divergent opinions as for broadcasting them rather than reserving them for his inner sanctum of friends. "Among friends," said Tito, "one can say anything in jest."

Djilas lost the friend who, after his older brother, had been his most important friend. He must have felt this painfully; perhaps that was why his behavior was so strange. It was almost as if he had irrevocably lost himself.

We know the consequences of his rapid fall, which was actually a new beginning for Djilas—a start that is still going on. Meanwhile, Djilas took new heart. Four months after the session mentioned above, he voluntarily left the Party. He commenced a new life articulated by periods of imprisonment; his books are the stages of a passionate search for freedom, which has stopped being a "petty bourgeois prejudice" for him. Freedom is the major theme for the Democratic Socialist Djilas became after the Hungarian October.

Of the two books published almost everywhere outside his homeland and the Communist countries, *The New Class* has become a sensational success. The book is, as the presumptuous subtitle indicates, an analysis of the Communist system. "Almost everything the reader will find in this book has already been expressed elsewhere," the author admits at the beginning.

The world justifiably praised the book and encouraged the writer who in Sremska Mitrovica, the prison of his youth, had to atone for daring to "think differently," as Rosa Luxemburg had once called it, and to write differently. The critics would have done the heretic a greater service, however, if they had made him realize that they hoped not so much for theoretical writings as for the description of his unique experiences: the memoirs of a former orthodox Stalinist who, at the peak of his power, rebelled against the fictions that were responsible for murdering freedom.

The Anatomy of a Morality was the title of a long essay that created a scandal and particularly aroused the indignation of the wives of the leading bureaucrats of Belgrade. Djilas (and subsequently the international press) overestimated the significance of the society affair treated in the article as well as the significance of the essay itself. It would certainly be important to write an *Anatomy of the Morality* of the various social strata ruled by the new class that claims to be Socialist or Communist. It would also be important to know the history of the moral development of a man like Djilas himself: the illegal Communist, the totalitarian inquisitor, the civil-war general, and finally the second-highest dignitary of a dictatorship—for Djilas was all these things. Neither Smyatin nor Victor Serge, Silone, Orwell, Koestler, nor their followers ever had the experiences Djilas could recount. By doing so, he could gain the support of certain Yugoslav intellectuals who so far have not forgiven him his aggressive intolerance. To receive their forgiveness he would have to ask for it.

If *Land without Justice,* his second book, was simply the first volume of an autobiography, the second volume may bring us the confessions that would ensure Djilas a more important niche in the literature of experience.

We know that he wrote a lengthy study of the life and works of Prince Negoš, the first Montenegrin poet. This book, too, was banned in Yugoslavia. Finally, on May 25, 1962, *Conversations with Stalin* appeared in New York; the response was enormous there and elsewhere.

After this book was announced, Yugoslavia passed a new law, which caused Djilas to be arrested a fourth time, on April 7, 1962. He was accused of acting against the interests of his country and serving as an "instrument of the Cold

War." The trial, in which Djilas was sentenced to a total of eight years' imprisonment, took place in secret despite violent protests by the defendant. The Yugoslavs were afraid that Djilas would reveal the paltriness of the accusation and become an accuser in his own right.

So much for the tragicomedy of this litigation. Every regime will find judges willing to serve it when it wishes to destroy its opponents legally, and Tito mistakenly resolved some years ago to force the law of silence upon his earlier apostle and friend. Why? To prevent him from disclosing state secrets? Nonsense: the greatest secret common to all regimes—that nations are governed with little intelligence—is a state secret that has been spreading for quite a while. No one has paid it the least attention.

Djilas had no secrets to betray. But an issue of the Italian magazine *Tempo Presente* was banned in Yugoslavia because it contained a short story that, according to the State Secretary for Domestic Affairs, "slandered the fight for national liberation as well as the leaders and the officers of the Army." This ban, published in the official gazette of Belgrade, refrains from mentioning the author of the short story —Milovan Djilas.

"The War" is an excellent short text and so far the surest sign of the writer's talent. Is it a chapter of a book in which the former general of the army of liberation describes his experiences? Is it an excerpt from his volume of confessions? The question remains open.

Why did the Yugoslav censor have to repress these few pages, which simply relate a tragic episode without mention of name, place, or time? It is claimed that the story reflects events that actually took place toward the end of the war. Young Serbs with no military preparation and almost without arms were thrown against battle-experienced German units who, under safe cover, effortlessly mowed down troop after troop of the recruits. Is this true? Who knows. . . .

Yet the ban remains a peculiar measure that demands explanation.

Some thirty years ago, Josip Broz declared before a Zagreb court that no emergency laws could bind him and that nothing could prevent him from acting in accordance with his conscience. Tito cannot completely have forgotten the young man he once was, nor can he have forgotten the true goals he fought for.

In the twilight hours in which the past overcomes the elderly man for long moments, President Tito has to admit to himself that the state whose immoderately lauded chief he is barely resembles the Socialist society for which Broz struggled until his fiftieth year. There *are* changes, including many improvements. But how many dead men, how much apocalyptic suffering preceded them? And once again there are emergency laws to deprive a man of his freedom only because his opinions differ; once again there are special police actions against a pitifully isolated heretic.

It may be that one of the Marshal's old friends, a writer perhaps, who once suffered greatly because of Super-Commissar Djilas and has since grown wise, will tell his friend Tito that there are many weighty reasons for *not* prosecuting the author of the little tale "The War." The man might say:

"Let the Montenegrin leave the country. He'll learn for himself that the world doesn't like heretics and despises the defeated, that the story of an exile is interesting for a moment and boring for an eternity.

"People may object that he could hurt your interests abroad. Impossible! At worst, he'll simply be reiterating what your old enemies have been spreading all this time without any effect. Don't forget that in prison Djilas, totally alone, could become a powerful, all-too-powerful opponent.

His power will be greatest when neither he nor any of us are still alive."

In Milovan Djilas's case, the main problem is not just himself but our era and every one of us, our right to think and to write as we please: against the real or alleged majorities, against rulers, Hitlers, Stalins, and the others, whether they are dead or still alive. Against the dictatorial lies and the ideological distortions—with no exceptions. And also against our own past and our own mistakes—in a word: against ourselves. Last but not least, our goal is the right to defend the victims because they are victims.

May 1, 1962

P.S. On December 31, 1966, Djilas was pardoned and released.

The Assassin

~~~~~~

FOREWORD

THE following essay was written just a few months after the publication of the Warren Report and appeared in the Parisian magazine **Preuves** *in March 1965. Since then many books and countless articles have concerned themselves with Lee Oswald as the sole culprit in the Kennedy assassination, or have seriously questioned whether he was guilty at all.*

Most of the authors took a decidedly skeptical if not hostile stance toward the Commission and at times scornfully rejected its findings. The majority tried to convince their readers that the murdered President had been the victim of a conspiracy.

Although I have carefully perused many of these writings, I still see no reason to alter even a line of my essay. Naturally there is no conclusive proof of Oswald's guilt—nor will there ever be any. Skepticism is always in order and in fact almost always more useful to intellectual integrity than dogmatic convictions.

"The Assassin" was not written to support any political or legal thesis. I was mainly interested in a problem which is central to all my thoughts and recurs in all my works: the re-

lationship between man and his actions. Proof that Oswald was not the assassin would detract nothing from the psychological essence of my observations. None of the authors, however, has offered any evidence against Oswald's guilt or any convincing proof that a conspiracy was actually afoot.

Five years after the assassination, there is still not a single trace of a political assassination—despite the chatter of professional exposers. These negative facts provide the Warren Report—which has been violently attacked for years—with greater validity than it could have had at the time it appeared.

For this reason, too, I have changed nothing in my essay.

Paris, April 1968

MORE than any so-called natural demise, each sudden death challengest the naïve futurist fiction to which we adjust all our techniques of living. Shaken for a few minutes, or for a sleepless night, or even for a few days, we have a hard time existing along the lines of normal habits—no longer sheltered by the "as if" of our sempiternal duration.

The violent death of someone close to us gives rise to plaguing questions which only the past could answer, if it weren't the past; and such a death reminds us, majestically and with tormenting insistence, that a single violent instant destroys all time: in a single moment a single drop swallows up an ocean and disappears along with it into the adjacent nothingness of our nightmares. Yet we will never resist the temptation to prolong the murderous moment with explanations that reintegrate it into our human time.

The often traumatic shock of a sudden loss seems at first to be essentially an emotional reaction, mingling compassion and the pain of bereavement, fear for oneself, and sometimes guilt—the result, according to Freudianism, of the long-suppressed desire to get rid of the person who has just died. These are joined, obviously, by a cheap sorrow whose intensity betrays in exact degree a contemptible satisfaction at not being identical with the dead man. One can also detect that invigorating excitement that attends catastrophes, victories, happy surprises, and all unexpected events. No amount of hypocrisy can hide the puerile enjoyment every interruption of routine affords to a humanity which, able to live only in its automatizing habits, never stops dreaming of the unusual.

All this is present in the archetypal shock inflicted by the death of an Achilles or a Siegfried. And one finds the same phenomena following the assassination of President Kennedy in Dallas—a murder that appalled and plunged into mourning the entire population of our planet. There, for the first time since the creation of the world, hundreds of millions of viewers were able to watch the fatal event unfolding over and over again on their television screens.

Never have so many men witnessed an assassination of this kind, the killing of the young leader of the most powerful nation on earth. But just as the conquered enemy never resembles the diabolical creature one thought one was fighting, the most destructive acts—squeezing the trigger of a rifle or dropping a bomb—seem mundane gestures compared with a violent blow, a powerfully hurled stone, or an attacking knife.

Consequently, the innumerable spectators, frustrated at the poor spectacle offered by the immense event, suspected they were being duped. Each thought to himself: "Impossible. That's no way to assassinate the leader of some 200 million men. And besides, who wanted to get rid of him? And why now, of all times? No, I saw it; it happened, but it's impossible."

Half an hour after the fatal shot the news was known by all, and everyone expected that hours and days would pass before anyone would manage to plumb the darkness that inevitably shrouded the crime. Since the visible part on television had been inadequate and disturbing, like an impassioned speaker whose words we cannot hear, it seemed that the assassination simply must have been the product of a formidable machination, hatched by villains with a true genius for dissimulation and a power made unfathomable by secret complicities and arcane connivances.

By nightfall of November 22, 1963, everyone knew that the murderer of the President had been arrested after committing another murder, and that the Dallas police were questioning him without interruption. Shortly thereafter, all television screens showed a rather odd-looking young man: Lee Harvey Oswald stared at the camera with amazement and a touch of irony, and apparently not without a certain scornful impatience. The prisoner's swollen eye was attributed to a punch by the policeman who had overpowered him as he again leveled the gun with which he had just killed J. D. Tippit, a policeman.

The alleged murderer remained the focus of public and media attention. From the very first, the Dallas police, both chiefs and subordinates, practiced a generous open-door policy toward one and all. The corridors through which Oswald was expected to pass never emptied day or night. Reporters, photographers, newsreel and television cameramen, as well as idlers, were constantly on the premises. They harassed him with questions every time he came by, labored along behind his escort, and wedged in among the mass of onlookers.

It has been said that the Dallas police feared accusations of negligence, if not of tacit or active complicity, and were allowing everyone in simply to prove that they had nothing to hide. This supposition is credible.

Furthermore, almost everyone had an urge for publicity, exacerbated by the unique opportunity to be seen and to show off before the millions of television viewers indefatigably watching and taking part in the investigation "as if they were right there." The Dallas tragedy and its aftermath allowed professional purveyors of information to achieve their goal at last: they could transmit the event itself and not just its shadow—not just the mere information that follows the event at a distance. And all of us were there two days later when Jack Ruby, hurling himself upon Oswald, shot him down with the greatest of ease.

Yes indeed, as of November 22 and during the subsequent days we could see everything; we could hear everything that the police, the real or alleged witnesses, the would-be experts, the journalists, politicians, philosophers, and stripteasers were willing to reveal. As a result, everything plunged deeper and deeper into confusion, except the psychological effect of the three murders. Anything seemed possible, but nothing was believable. And common sense warned everyone of the deception he was about to fall victim to.

As common sense would have it, the assassination of the President of the United States was a political act if ever there was one. In comparison with this enormous fact, Lee Harvey Oswald weighed less than a feather. The instrument of a giant machine, that's what this ex-marine must be—unless, of course, he had no hand at all in the matter. Or else he was a very important agent of the American, Russian, Cuban secret service—and so forth.

Since the excellent reputation of common sense is by definition unassailable, one can easily see how common sense will serve to justify the worst stupidities and the most noxious aberrations when applied to matters less reasonable than it requires. Common sense alone overlooks the fact that human nature deceives it unabashedly.

As soon as it was learned that Lee Harvey Oswald had spent a few years in the Soviet Union and come back with a Russian wife, right-wingers proclaimed that they knew all they had to know: the crime was signed by the Communists —in fact, by the entire Left, and indirectly by the victim himself. And they reminded everyone that they had never stopped reproaching the late President for his weakness toward the forces of disintegration. When it came out a few hours later that the accused had gone, or tried to go, to Havana two months before and had headed the local New Orleans section of the Fair Play for Cuba Committee, a dazzling light blinded the right-wingers. Oswald had incontestably been an agent for Castro, assigned to punish Kennedy for issuing the famous ultimatum to Khrushchev in October 1962, and to impose a pro-Castro policy on America.

Countless people, on both the Right and the Left, who had despised Kennedy and condemned his politics, discovered that in their heart of hearts they were profoundly affected by his death. From this they concluded that they had always cared for him, and that only their enemies could have killed him.

The leftists cried out that the pro-Communist appearance of the suspect's past obviously and irrefutably proved this to be a right-wing crime, committed by segregationist reactionaries, the John Birch Society, the American Fact-Finding Committee (which, the very morning of the crime, had welcomed the President by inserting an ad in the *Dallas Morning News,* consisting of twelve questions which were actually perfidious insinuations), and, finally, by Texas multimillionaires, owners of oilfields, and so many others.

Although thirteen months earlier the pro-Castro Left had been accusing Kennedy of acting like Hitler and being a war criminal, after the assassination the very same people were, and were to remain, the most fervent mourners and most stubborn partisans of the idea that the President had fallen victim to a dark conspiracy of racists, anti-Castroites, and warmongers.

Neither of these two symmetrical interpretations completely ignored Oswald: he had served as an instrument, along with so many others, in a plot as vast as it was diabolical. Jack Ruby's gunshots were convenient evidence that he, like Oswald, was in the service of that tentacular organization.

All these theses, presented to the public as pertinent evidence, all these speculations and imputations were cited and refuted in "Speculations and Rumors" (Appendix XII) in the *Report of the President's Commission on the Assassination of President John F. Kennedy*. These 880 pages make up an exceptionally valuable document; they reflect an admirable honesty in establishing certain facts as well as in admitting uncertainties and doubts. There remain other doubts—mainly those provoked by the procedures of the Dallas police, but also such uncertainties as arise concerning the attempted assassination of E. A. Walker. (This will be discussed below.)

The conclusion of this document, commonly known as the "Warren Report" (and sure to count as one of the best books of our time), holds no interest for the greater public, which finds so much to intrigue it elsewhere, nor for the conspiracy and espionage experts, nor for the sensationalists.* For, after verifying all the direct and indirect testimonies, examining all the hypotheses, and tracing the suspicions back to their sources; after weighing the actual importance of the political ambiance in the nation and particularly in Dallas, where long before the fatal day the hatred for President Kennedy

---

* Before the publication of the Warren Report, one of these specialists offered to furnish its editors, within two weeks after publication, with a text proving the inexactness of the statements and conclusions of the Presidential Commission.

and his collaborators (Adlai Stevenson, for example) had exploded ignobly; after investigating all the biographical material liable to illuminate the personalities of Lee Harvey Oswald and Jack Ruby, the Warren Commission concluded that Oswald had committed the assassination on his own, without a conspiracy or even accomplices; but that there still remained a number of unexplained psychological contradictions and effects disproportionate with their known causes.

The crime was, so to speak, a "monological act," in that its basic determinants were psychological, and social only to the extent that each man is a "social whole" (Marx). Consequently, this assassination must have been totally gratuitous, unmotivated, and ineffective—despite its terrible outcome.

The disturbing thing about a case of this sort is the overlapping of two frames of reference, one referring to the destiny of our planet, and the other to the sickness of an isolated person, incapable of enduring or transcending his mediocrity but capable of murder.

We should, if possible, know and understand the case of Lee Harvey Oswald. Unique as he is, he resembles many others who ultimately remain in the background unnoticed.

Lee Harvey Oswald was born in New Orleans, Louisiana, on October 18, 1939, two months after the death of his father, a collector in an insurance company. His mother had had a son by her first husband, whom she left after two years of marriage. Robert, her elder son by her second husband, was five and a half years older than Lee. Marguerite Claviere was remarried in Dallas in 1945 and divorced in 1948 on the grounds that she was "guilty of excesses, cruelty and outrages." Since his brothers lived for long periods in children's homes, Lee enjoyed the privileges of being an only child, even though he too spent thirteen months in a home, when he was three. Over and over again, it was Lilian Murret, his mother's sister, who took care of the child. Oswald and his mother must have moved twenty times before he finally left her.

From his birth until his death at twenty-four, Oswald's existence was that of a vagabond. Neither the child nor the adolescent was ever offered the least chance to establish roots; there was no place he could consider his home. He was always on the move, as if perpetually fleeing—forward, he must have thought. It was merely a movement in a narrow circle. By running to the point of exhaustion, one thinks he can conquer the infinite, but wherever he may stop it is never far from the point of departure.

His decision to join the Marine Corps before he had reached the legal age of seventeen impelled him to write a letter, to which he signed his mother's name, informing the school that he was moving. This terminated his schooling. A few days after his sixteenth birthday he appeared at the recruitment office with a false affidavit, supposedly from his mother, certifying that he was seventeen years old. He was rejected and had to wait another year. While waiting, he worked as a messenger and an office boy; during his leisure hours he would read the *Marine Manual,* which his brother Robert had lent him, and books from the library—notably Communist writings, as it appears. Three weeks before his induction, on October 26, 1956, he wrote to the Socialist Workers' Party to ask if that organization had a young people's section at Fort Worth, where he was living at the time. "I'm a Marxist," he wrote; "I've been studying Socialist principles for more than fifteen months."

Nothing came of this letter, nor of most of his other overtures. Oswald never managed to join any organized group or party; he never belonged to any community except the more imagined than real one of a barrack or a military section. But it was not a community that the impatient volunteer was seeking in the service. What then? First of all, it was probably an equality with his brothers, both of whom had been marines. More importantly, the prestige attached to this elite corps, so famous for its toughness and daring, must have attracted him. Lee, malingering, shy, lonely, with no particular talents and no diplomas, could hope that the marine uniform would transform him into an important and courageous man, that material independence would free him once and for all from his mother's tutelage, and, finally, that he would be sent on long trips to exotic countries full of seductive women that he, too, might easily seduce.

Essentially, things happened just as the adolescent had dreamed they would. He traveled a good deal, both in America and the Pacific, for he was assigned to radar stations near Tokyo, Japan, and in the Philippines. Although a disciplined soldier, Lee was court-martialed twice—once because a gun that he had hidden in his locker had gone off, wounding him slightly (personal ownership of arms was forbidden in the service), and a few months later for getting drunk and insulting a noncommissioned officer. He lost his first-class rank.

In February 1959, he took an examination in Russian, a language he had studied on his own, but insufficiently; he flunked. For a long time beforehand he had been telling his buddies how interested he was in everything Russian and how sympathetic he was toward the Soviet Union. They called him "Oswaldkovich," which seemed to flatter him. He felt he was finally becoming a man of note, distinguished from everyone else by his interest in international politics and his affinity for Russia and Cuba. He had a copy of *Das Kapital*, as well as the wildly anti-Stalinist books of George Orwell. He liked to be seen holding a Russian newspaper and talking about Marxism, in which he claimed to be an expert, amid young soldiers incapable of judging his claims and totally indifferent to them.

All in all, his three years in the Marine Corps must have been among the happiest of his life. It was probably his most stable period and a source of encouragement to him. Some six months before it ended he wrote to the Albert Schweitzer *collège* in Switzerland, applying for admission in 1960. Beyond the deliberate inaccuracies and untruths, his *curriculum vitae* is astonishing for its inarticulateness and its peculiar spelling. He lists Jack London, Charles Darwin, and Norman Vincent Peale as his three favorite authors and gives his vocation as writing short stories.

On September 4, 1959, a week before his service was up, he applied for a passport, declaring his intention to study in Switzerland and Finland and to travel to certain other countries: Cuba, England, France, Germany, and Russia. He received his passport with no unusual delay.

Then he visited his mother in Fort Worth and told her he had decided to work on a ship, since that would be the best way to earn a lot of money. At the New Orleans travel agency he claimed to be a "maritime export agent" going on a holiday cruise. There was no problem about his paying the $220 for the ticket to Le Havre, for he had saved about $1,500 dollars from his pay.

Before sailing, he wrote to his mother, "My values are totally different from yours or Robert's.... I never spoke to you about my projects because I could never hope that you would understand."

Oswald left Le Havre the very day he arrived, and sailed to Southampton, where he claimed he wished to spend a week before going on to Switzerland. Actually, a few hours later, he went off to Helsinki. The Soviet visa, which he had obtained without difficulty, limited his residence in the Soviet

Union to six days. Upon getting off the train in Moscow on October 6, he was taken over by Intourist.

An intimate journal, which Oswald called his *Historic Diary,* gives a detailed account of the dramatic events during his first few weeks in the Soviet Union and a day-by-day report on his later experiences as a metallurgy worker in Minsk.

The ex-marine lost no time in telling his young Intourist guide of his resolve to make an immediate break with his own country, remain in Russia and become a Russian citizen. Dumbfounded, she quickly reported this to the proper authority and was ordered to help Oswald present his case and apply to the Supreme Soviet for naturalization. On October 19, a reporter for Radio Moscow questioned him for a long time in his hotel room. It was probably a police interrogation, and the conclusion must have been that the young American was fairly uninteresting; for, a few hours after the official interview at the visa office, Oswald was told to leave Moscow without further delay. The Intourist employee who came to see him found him in a dead faint: he had opened the veins on his left arm.

Brought to the hospital, Oswald was detained for a mental examination. He now claimed that he regretted his action and wanted to return to his native land. But, when summoned to the visa office after his recovery, he again affirmed his resolution to become a Soviet citizen. He was told to exercise patience. For three days and three nights he waited at the telephone in his room, without eating or sleeping, but in vain.

The afternoon of October 31, a Saturday, he went to the American consulate. No sooner had he stepped into the vestibule than he dropped his passport at the receptionist's window and said he wanted to "dissolve" his American citizenship. The consul was alerted and invited Oswald into his office, where the excited visitor presented him with a written request for the "revocation" of his American nationality, explaining that he had come to the Soviet Union, the only country he felt any bond with, to be naturalized. As in his shipboard conversations, Oswald spoke about his mother's poverty, the poverty of a working woman. He said he had made up his mind never to suffer such poverty. On the other hand, he accused the Marine Corps of failing to give him the rank he deserved. Finally, he condemned American imperialism and assured the consul that he would reveal to the Soviets all he had managed to learn during his military service —notably the secret details of radar control. The consul asked Oswald to think it over until Monday; on that day, he could carry out all the formalities.

But Oswald never came, thus refusing to renounce his nationality through required formal procedure. A few days later, however, he wrote to the embassy, complaining that he had been denied the legal right to "revoke" his citizenship. The moment he became a Soviet citizen, he announced, he would demand that "his" government address a formal protest to the United States. The immediate reply informed Oswald that he could come to the consulate during office hours to settle his case, and that was all; the documents he had to sign were awaiting him there. But Oswald responded neither to this letter nor to any subsequent notice of the kind.

His behavior in this extremely important matter is characteristic: although the motives behind his aggressiveness survive, his enthusiasm exhausts itself in an initial violent action and he remains as far from his goal as before. While waiting for his spirit to revive, he tends to forget or to distort his memory of the action he has undertaken with such unshakable resolution. "I'll never go back to the U.S.A, a country I hate," he wrote in early November to his brother

Robert, who had been reading newspapers for details of his younger brother's loud defection. Evidently Lee was aware that his story had made the front pages, as he had foreseen and hoped. However, other events he had banked on came about less speedily. The Russians—who should have naturalized him the day after his shattering break with his imperialist native land and put him in the limelight as an ex-marine who, "choosing liberty," asked only to reveal the hideous face of empire, etc.—the Russians held their peace. They let him cool his heels in his hotel room, where he remained completely isolated except for the American journalists who petitioned him for interviews. Finally giving in, he agreed to see Aline Mosby, a reporter for the United Press. In everything he said to her, and later to Priscilla Johnson, another American correspondent, Lee Oswald mixed truth, half-truths, and lies, unconvincingly.

He claimed he had been interested in communism since he was fifteen years old, when an old lady in the streets of New York had handed him a leaflet demanding an appeal of sentence for the Rosenbergs. In fact, Lee was only fourteen years old when the couple was executed. Since he had offered his Marxist convictions as his reason for deciding to remain in the Soviet Union, Priscilla Johnson asked him to name the authors he had read between the ages of fifteen and twenty. He recalled only two names, Marx and Engels, and only one title: *Das Kapital.*

For nearly a century this has been the habitual reply of ignorant chatterers who believe there is no risk in bragging this way before indifferent illiterates. And Oswald had gotten used to posing as an expert Marxist before an audience incapable of testing him. He was faithful to this practice until his death: declaring to the policemen who interrogated him in Dallas that he was a Marxist but not a Marxist-Leninist, he refused to explain the difference between the two because "it would take too much time." And he added that he had read practically everything written by and about Karl Marx.

His *Historic Diary,* like his letters and his statements, demonstrates that he had picked up only the flattest phraseology from the most banally sectarian tracts and newspaper articles. His technique of lying was that of an unintelligent child or a mediocre and unstable adolescent, presuming always that forgetfulness and indolence will keep others from verifying what he says. Paranoiacs, so readily suspicious of everybody and everything, infallibly count on being trusted by others.

January 4, 1960, not naturalized but recognized as stateless, Oswald finally obtained an identity card and permission to reside in Russia for a year; he also received the sum of 5,000 ancient rubles—half of which was to cover his hotel bill. And he was asked to come to Minsk. There he was hospitably welcomed by the mayor, who, in addition to a warm reception, gave him a place to stay far superior to that of his co-workers in the factory.

He lived quite comfortably, for besides his worker's pay he received a monthly sum of 700 rubles, an unexplained allotment by an organization disguised as a branch of the Russian Red Cross. His origin was a social advantage for Oswald, and his privileged situation made him even more interesting in that he could invite his acquaintances to the theater, the cafe, and so forth. As a member of a hunting association, he spent a dozen weekends in the country, where he seems to have been struck by the poverty of the peasants and the neglect in the villages.

Ella, a Polish girl with whom he had fallen in love, turned him down, and so he married Marina Prusakova four months later. The day after his wedding he wrote that he had married Marina to get back at Ella, and, later, he added that the "transition of changing his full love for Ella to Marina was very painful." All his expressions are deformed by an artificial style, even when they reflect real suffering.

In early February 1961, fifteen months after his arrival in the U.S.S.R., he asked the American Embassy to return his passport and stated his desire to go back to the United States. He concludes, "I hope you will remember your responsibility towards America just as I remember mine, and that you will do everything to help me because I am an American citizen."

With the beginning of this correspondence—which led to Oswald's repatriation, accompanied by his wife and child—his monthly allotment stopped. From then on his condition was far more like that of most Russian workers, and he admitted without reticence that the Soviet reality was quite different from his former image of it.

When he landed in a port near New York, some thirty months after sailing from New Orleans, his meager baggage contained several manuscripts. Altogether, there were fifty to sixty pages, comprising a synopsis of his disappointing experiences in Minsk, an anti-Russian and anti-American manifesto, a declaration he intended to read to the journalists who would welcome him on arrival, and, finally, two distinct versions—parts of which were diametrically opposed—of an interview he was preparing for the press. He foresaw questions; and yet, even at the end of the second version, the journalists would say, "Thank you very much, Mr. Oswald. You are a true patriot!"

He was twenty-two years and ten months old; he had only seventeen months left to live in obscurity before dying before the eyes of the entire world.

Since the age of sixteen he had considered himself a Marxist; and, although shaken by what he had seen and experi-

enced in the "homeland of socialism," he remained faithful
to his "principles." But what were they? And what had
started the adolescent on that road?

It wasn't material poverty, for he had never had to suffer
it. After the death of his father the family sold their house at
a profit; later the mother always earned enough to cover the
needs of her children, and certainly those of her youngest.
She had never been the poor working woman her son cited
as an exemplary victim of capitalist exploitation. A commer-
cial clerk whose services were justly valued, she earned adequate salaries; but she moved and changed jobs too often,
and thus prevented her son from ever knowing a stable
home. She took him to New York where he was the "South-
erner," exuberantly made fun of; and he suffered so much
from it that he finally avoided going to school, but spent his
days walking, to the point of exhaustion, down the long ave-
nues of the immense city that was so different from New Orleans. Then, back in his native city, he was ridiculed for his
Yankee speech, whose accent he probably exaggerated.

No, it wasn't economic poverty that inspired his wish to
be a Marxist; it was a discovery he must have made while
reading the newspapers, which at that time made frequent
reference to Marxists and Reds in their denunciations of
Communists, including socialists and left-wingers in general.
McCarthy's Manichaeanism—less powerful and, for that reason, more visibly preposterous than that of ruling fascist or
Communist totalitarians—was manufacturing that chain of
identifications which transformed the real or alleged adver-
sary into a terrifyingly powerful and ubiquitous demon.

This image of diabolical Marxists corresponded to the
idea, widely held in Europe, of a Soviet Marxism that had
won the hearts of the intelligentsia, especially in Italy and
France between the resistance and occupation. Proudly proclaiming their submission to the "law of history," they would

declare themselves Marxists and—like Oswald—cite all sorts of prestigious readings, which actually were unnecessary, since they had made up their minds *a priori,* and boring, since in fact they weren't interested in political economy, or history, or the factional quarrels of yesteryear.

Young Lee felt different from those around him, and he had all but abandoned the effort to resemble the heroes proclaimed by his peers. He never took part in athletic contests; there was nothing likable or impressive about him. Moreover, he was often a bad student and would play hooky to escape day-by-day failure.

It was probably during his unhappy time in New York that he became convinced that he was different from other people and that he was unable to change this. Feelings of this sort, born from a humiliating sense of inferiority, are almost inevitably overcompensated, transformed into a feeling of superiority so great as to give rise to an autistic allophobia that the deranged individual applies to himself in schizoid exasperation.

On the one hand, Oswald decided to join the Marine Corps as soon as possible and, while still an adolescent, to become as hard and tough as possible. On the other hand, having discovered the negative or anti-hero of Marxism (in the midst of global confusion, as the McCarthyist mythology presented him), Oswald had one of those revelations that change a life in a single instant: he would declare himself a Marxist and thus become a superior being—immediately, without great effort, and without depending on anything else whatsoever.

He had never met a Marxist; he knew no Socialists or Communists. He knew nothing whatever about the history of the workers' movement, parties, or trade unions; but he knew that the Marxists, a tiny minority in his country, were formidable people, fearful and feared. He borrowed books by Marx, very probably the three volumes of *Das Kapital*, since that title is listed in all reference works. Wherever he went he would borrow volumes of Marx and sometimes works by Engels, as well as—probably—Darwin and Ingersoll. But he never read them. He had not acquired the habit of reading books, and he died without acquiring it. His vocabularly was heavily dependent on the clichés regularly furnished by *The Worker* (the newspaper of the American Communist Party), *The Militant* (the organ of the Socialist Workers' Party), and other periodicals of that kind. He knew nothing about past and present battles, nothing about the great conflicts of our time, and he seemed unaware of the social, economic, and political events that continue to shape his country.

Living among the people of Minsk, he could observe a great deal that eludes foreign tourists. But his critique remains superficial; for although he discovered the rôle of the Bolshevik Party, he never really understood it. The authority exercised by party functioneers in the factory revolted him, but he never even suspected the network and machinery at the disposal of this power, whose ideological claims no longer deceive anyone in the U.S.S.R.

On the boat that brought him back he wrote that neither American capitalism nor Russian communism is acceptable, and that a third way would have to be found. But at this point he loses himself in a pitiful verbiage, for he knows nothing.

Nevertheless, his paranoid rapport with truth allowed him to believe his own sincerity and courage and to consider himself a Marxist when he prepared the following two answers to questions he thought the journalists were certain to ask him: "Are you a Communist?" Reply number 1: "*Yes, basically yes.* Although I hate the U.S.S.R. and the Socialist system, I still think that Marxism can produce results in different circumstances." Reply number 2: *"No, obviously not.* I've never even met a Communist, except in the Soviet Union where you can't avoid it." And so forth.

Neither the Dr. Jekyll nor the Mr. Hyde interview became known, because no one came to meet the returning marine except a representative of a philanthropic society. With the help of this society and of his brother Robert, Lee was able to fly to Dallas with his wife and his son, and was then taken to Fort Worth. The same local newspapers that had trumpeted his deeds and gestures when he had noisily broken with Moscow now ignored his existence. Oswald, repatriated and regarding himself as a political figure of national and international proportions, was prepared to buck ferocious adversaries, but once again he found himself plunged into obscurity. Thus it became urgent that he publish his book on Russia as soon as possible, although in fact he had no more than a few dozen pages. The typist who had prepared some of them recommended it to a professor of Russian, who she thought might give Oswald some material aid. Thanks to this man and his son, who took Russian lessons from Marina, the family was welcomed into a community of Russian-Americans. These new friends were particularly drawn to the young wife; they took pity on her poverty and suffering at the side of a husband who was unable to offer her a comfortable life and who brutalized her, in all likelihood because he didn't really care enough for her.

Among these people Marina could unbosom herself: She soon grew to hate her husband, who clearly would never succeed—not even in sex, as she seems to have reproached him brutally in front of their friends. Oswald once again became estranged from his mother and forbade Marina to let her visit them in their apartment. Then he broke with the Russians, who kept encouraging his wife to leave him.

He found mediocre, badly paid jobs, which he left or

quickly lost. As in his childhood, he moved around too much and found roots nowhere. In the year following his return he moved no less than eight times.

He subscribed to *The Worker* and *The Militant;* he often wrote to the Communist Party, to certain of its parallel committees, and to the Socialist Workers' Party, which he wanted to join. He rarely got any answers to his requests for information and offers of collaboration as a newspaperman and photographer. No one ever asked him for anything. His address for mail, newspapers, and other printed matter was P.O. Box 2915 in Dallas, from October 9, 1962, and P.O. Box 3061 in New Orleans as of June 11. He wrote to the post office that that box would be used by Lee H. Oswald, Marina Oswald, and A. J. Hidell.

Alek James Hidell, who once turned into Dr. J. A. Hideel to sign a false vaccination certificate, appeared during winter 1962–63—probably in January. Oswald, working in a graphics firm, took advantage of a bit of technological know-how he had acquired and forged two identity documents; made out for Alek James Hidell, they contained Oswald's own description and photograph. He ordered fire-arms by mail: on January 27, a Smith-Wesson .38-caliber revolver and, on March 12, a Mannlicher-Carcano rifle from Klein's Sporting Goods, Chicago. He signed the two orders A. Hidell and had the merchandise delivered to P.O. Box 2915.

The name Alek had been given him by his coworkers at the factory in Minsk, and, according to Marina Oswald, the name Hidell was chosen because it rhymed with Fidel. It is more probable that the pseudonym was derived through one of those wiles often involved in the choice of a *nom de guerre. Hide-L,* or, even more plainly, *Hide-eel:* Hide Lee.

With Hidell, Oswald began a new, second existence, clandestine and far superior to that of the insignificant, unspecialized hireling, the obscure man with no future.

Certain adolescents who feel outrageously misunderstood

by those around them and jeered by a stupid humanity sometimes take refuge in a second existence, an enclave of dreams
as consoling as the threat of vengeful suicide.

It is conceivable that during the summer of 1958, after his
second court-martial, Lee Oswald hit upon the idea, if not a
specific project, for an astounding action, a supreme exploit
that would justify the singularity of his person. The newspaper reports of defections—glorifying for a day or a week a
Soviet who chose liberty—showed Oswald one road he
might take. He started learning Russian, and, after his discharge from the marines, he chose Soviet liberty. From then
on he carrried a secret that added a new dimension to his existence as a second-class soldier. He alone knew that he was a
turncoat in power, a rebel who would betray the military secrets of his country and proclaim to the whole world that he
hated America and loved the Soviet Union, to which nation
alone he owed allegiance. Thus he found compensation for a
wounded ego and frustrated ambitions in a solipsistic joy
like that of the dwarf in Grimm's fairy tale, who cries out to
the four winds, "Oh, how happy I am that no one knows my
name is Rumpelstiltzkin!"

But the Moscow experiment failed; the Russians considered him politically unimportant—and Oswald never understood why. His stay in Minsk, disappointing in every way,
probably only weakened his dominant fantasy without destroying it. This fantasy, more necessary and obsessive than
ever, revived six months after his depressing return from the
Soviet Union; now it was embodied in Alek Hidell.

Hidell bought weapons—why? Perhaps for no special reason; but, in any event, it gave Oswald the feeling that he
could do momentous things if and when he *wanted to*. This
potential for destruction, of which he was the sole master, set
the tone of his second existence and made his everyday life
almost bearable. He lived again, as he had in the months

preceding his Soviet adventure, in what might be called "the *secret of the iceberg"*: the exposed emerging part looks deceptively insignificant; yet the invisible part is gigantic and inexorable, destroying all who are unaware of it.

There are many Hidells living among us in a mixture of oppressive anguish and bad hope. Trembling, they await a supreme humiliation, which they will avenge by an irremediable act. But ordinarily they fail here, too, just as they fail in their daily lives, their loves, and their suicides.

As soon as the mail-order weapons arrived, Oswald posed with them for a photograph, holding his two favorite newspapers. He intended to send the photo to *The Militant* at the proper moment. Oswald envisioned killing General Edwin A. Walker, who, as head of an extreme right-wing movement, was stirring up a lot of dust, especially in his home town, Dallas. On the evening of April 10, 1963, a gunshot through his window just barely missed him.

There are reasons for suspecting Oswald. That very day, April 10, he had left his wife a note anticipating some extraordinary event in whose wake he would be dead or imprisoned. There are photos of Walker's house that Oswald took with his own camera, and Oswald's memo book contains the ex-general's address and telephone number.

Finally, he is supposed to have admitted to Marina that he shot at Walker. But there is no definite proof. All we can tell for certain is that in early April he was planning an astounding action with consequences he could not foresee. Nevertheless, the psychologist hesitates simply to accept a version based essentially on Marina Oswald's testimony. It is probable that Lee had only toyed with the idea of killing Walker, but that after losing his job on April 6, Hidell had been compelled to act. He may have written the note in question on the tenth, perhaps earlier; but after the attempted

murder of Walker he acted as if he were the culprit. Someone else may have preempted him. If so, it was one of those
ironic farces that furnish the boarders of Olympus with their
daily distractions. (We shall see more of these divine practical jokers in full action.)

The possibility that Oswald really fired and then fled after
the first shot is not to be categorically excluded. This might
explain his decision to leave Dallas, in order to escape possible investigation.

The work he found in New Orleans barely interested
him, and, having managed to collect large sums of back un-
employment insurance, he contemplated devoting himself
entirely to political activity in case he lost his job.

He wrote to the Fair Play for Cuba Committee in New
York, first of all to get a membership card. Then he wrote to
its secretary general several times, to tell him, among other
things, about the creation of a local chapter of the Committee in New Orleans, but he waited in vain for an answer and
encouragement. Under the name Lee Osborne, he had some
small pamphlets printed and stuck labels on them, some
bearing his real name and address, others the name A. J. Hidell and the P.O. box he had rented in New Orleans. The
essential text of the pamphlet was: "Hands off Cuba! Join
the Fair Play for Cuba Committee. . . . Everyone welcome!"
In June he began distributing these pamphlets near the harbor, and later, after he lost his job, in other parts of town,
sometimes with the help of teenagers he paid by the hour.
All his efforts remained ineffectual and infinitely remote
from the results he boasted of in his letters to the New York
Committee.

He announced that the New Orleans section, presided
over by A. J. Hidell, already had thirty-five members, as well
as an office and a meeting place. A bit later he claimed that
the proprietor had closed down the meeting place for politi-

cal reasons and under transparent pretexts. Oswald made a big thing of his vast activity, the mass of letters pouring in, and he complained about the lack of a secretary. He said he had been handing out thousands of pamphlets. None of this was true. And once again everything he had undertaken was threatening to evaporate before attracting any attention, when a rather irritating incident finally seemed to open the great door for him. A Cuban exile to whom he had introduced himself as an anti-Castroist in order to get information caught him distributing pro-Castro leaflets and violently attacked him. A policeman took the two men to the police station, but there would have been no repercussions if a reporter hadn't gotten his hands on the story. He broadcast a five-minute interview with Oswald on the radio, then, four days later, a debate in which Oswald defended the Castroist point of view. As usual Oswald counted on the short memory of others, and that was why he was caught off-guard when he was reproachfully reminded of his Russian past and his propaganda was linked with his Communist commitment.

Following his interview, Oswald informed the Committee's secretary general that after the great success of his fifteen-minute program he was besieged by people wanting to join the Committee and inundated with invitations to take part in public debates. Oswald was anticipating an immense success in the coming radio debate, which would turn out badly for him; he was neither besieged nor inundated; only one visitor had come for information—an agent of the anti-Castroist organization.

It was another debacle. Oswald had to admit it to himself. He asked the New York Communist Party for advice: what should he do now that the notoriety of his past and his anti-American statements in Moscow militated against his heading the Fair Play for Cuba Committee? The intelligent answer he received was fairly useless, since he had been maintaining the fiction of an existent organization. He was advised to keep in the background—but whose background? There was no one but Oswald.

Nevertheless, he thought he had finally made a breakthrough out of obscurity. In 1959 the ex-marine had had no political experience that might have legitimized him; but thanks to his activity in New Orleans, after all the claimed accomplishments of his letters to New York, and particularly after his defense of Castro's position in a radio talk, he felt he had become someone—at least in the eyes of those he was going to join in a second "operation Moscow," developing in Havana in 1963.

When his wife and child went to stay with a friend in Irving, a suburb of Dallas, Oswald took a bus to Mexico City, arriving on September 27. Without delay he presented himself at the Cuban consulate, where he eloquently spoke of his merits, stressing his eminent role in the Fair Play for Cuba Committee. He showed newspaper clippings, and Russian personal documents to prove he was a member of the Communist Party. He claimed to be en route to the U.S.S.R. and asked for a transit visa; it was refused because he didn't have a Soviet visa. He was treated with indifference if not distrust, and when he insisted more vehemently the consul told him he was more detrimental than useful to the Cuban Revolution.

After five days of vain effort Oswald went back to Dallas, a beaten man. Obscurity awaited him, as well as marital and material difficulties—his wife was about to have their second baby. But things went more smoothly than he had anticipated. For, thanks to Mrs. Paine, the helpful friend who was lodging the family, he found work at the Texas School Book Depository, to begin October 16. Although it was a badly paid white-collar job, Oswald took heart. Once again he rented a P.O. box, where he might receive mail for the Fair Play for Cuba Committee, as well as the American Civil Liberties Union—the latter, because he had accompanied Mrs. Paine's husband to a single meeting of that organization. He also wrote again to an official of the New York Communist Party, to inform him of a Walkerist meeting he had attended, and to the Soviet embassy to apply for a visa for himself and his family. This second letter contained the medley of untruths characteristic of Oswald.

No. Despite everything, he did not abandon his headlong flight; the frenzied race within a pitifully narrow circle went on. It is not certain whether he really wanted to return to Russia or to continue his political "career." An F.B.I. agent, informed of his activity in New Orleans and his trip to Mexico, came to Irving to get information. Like the Russian agencies and, later, the Cuban, the F.B.I., which had been interested in Oswald since his return from Russia, concluded that the young man was neither dangerous nor useful, but merely a crank.

Lee spent his weekends with his family in Irving. He commuted in a car belonging to Buell W. Frazier, a coworker who lived in the same suburb. In Dallas Oswald resided in a kind of furnished hotel room, where he had registered under the name of O. H. Lee. His use of a pseudonym touched off a fight with his wife when, trying to telephone him, she was told there was no Oswald in the house. It was during the first weekend (November 16 and 17) that her husband had not spent at home; the Paine family was celebrating a birthday, and Lee would have been unwelcome.

On Thursday, November 21, Oswald went to Irving with Frazier to look for some curtain rods, which he said he needed for his room. His wife received him coolly, not yet having forgiven him after their quarrel; and besides, they hadn't expected him until the next day, Friday evening, as was customary. The couple spent the night without making up, even though Lee tried to get back into Marina's good graces with promises of a washing machine, an apartment, and so on.

The next morning he drove back with Frazier; he had put a large paper bag, supposedly containing curtain rods, in the back of the car. He was lying: he hadn't come to Irving for curtain rods; he didn't have any, nor has any trace of them ever been found. He had come to get the rifle Hidell had ordered on March 12, which had been hidden for some time in Mrs. Paine's garage. And it was with the Mannlicher Carcano-C 2766 that he returned to Dallas on Friday, November 22, 1963, in Frazier's car. He immediately put the rifle away in an upper story of the Book Depository.

The same day, at twelve-thirty, that rifle fired the bullets that mortally wounded President Kennedy. The Mannlicher Carcano-C 2766, with a telescopic sight, was found on the sixth floor, near the window from which the fatal shots had been fired. The identity of that rifle with the one ordered by Oswald under the name A. Hidell is thus as incontestable as the fact that the same Oswald was in the building before and during the assassination, and three minutes later when he was identified by Roy Truly, a senior clerk who was accompanying police officer M. L. Baker and met Oswald in the refreshment bar.

Not losing an instant, Oswald left the premises, took a bus, then got off to continue in a taxi until he reached the neighborhood of his home. After several minutes he came out of the house dressed in a zippered jacket. A bit later, at 1:16 P.M., police officer J. D. Tippit stopped his radio patrol car to investigate a passer-by and was killed by the person, who fired several revolver shots at him and then fled.

The murderer's path led past a parking lot—where Oswald's jacket was discovered. Attracting attention by his suspicious movements—obvious attempts to keep under cover —Lee Oswald was reported to the police by two people, one of them the cashier of the movie theater in which he was thrown down, disarmed, and arrested. The gun he aimed at the policeman was the one he had ordered on January 27, 1963, under the name Hidell. Ballistics experts considered it possible that Tippit's mortal wounds had been caused by bullets from this revolver, but they were not absolutely certain.

Oswald, who had said nothing upon running into Truly and Baker and then his cleaning woman, who spoke to him when she saw him entering the house, broke his silence in the presence of his interrogators. He instantly named the lawyer he intended to retain as his defense attorney: John Abt. There is no reason to assume that any kind of relations existed between Oswald and the New York attorney, whose name is well-known to readers of *The Worker* because of the long trial in which he defended the leaders of the American Communist Party.

All attempts by Oswald and his friends to telephone the lawyer were of no avail. While waiting to reach Abt, or at least to have an attorney assigned by the American Civil Liberties Union, the defendant categorically refused every offer made by the Dallas bar.

He denied everything—everything except leaving the bus and taking a taxi home. And even that he admitted only when told that the driver had already testified. He couldn't deny owning the revolver he was holding when arrested; he refused to explain why he had needed it or where he bought it. Nor could he deny having among his personal papers a false military I.D. card with his description and photo but bearing the name Alek James Hidell. When the police

insisted he explain what the card was for and why he had
forged it, he declared that he had nothing to say until he
could have the lawyer of his choosing.

He was charged on November 22, at 7:10 P.M., with murdering police officer J. D. Tippit, and only at 1:35 A.M., on
November 23, with assassinating the President. At a press
conference televised before midnight Oswald announced that
he didn't know what they were talking about, and that no
one had ever interrogated him about the death of Kennedy.

I saw Oswald on television screens; I heard and heard
again everything he said. He made me doubt his guilt.
There were certainly a great number of us in the world,
especially after Oswald's death, who recalled his statements
and the decisive way he had made them. We trembled at
the thought that this poor young man with his swollen
eye might actually have been the victim of a series of
misunderstandings, which a third murder had now made
irreparable.

And I kept my doubts until the appearance of the
Warren Report. After perusing those 880 pages with utmost
attention, and reading all the biographical documentation
over and over again, I know that Lee Oswald, a not-so-
innocent persecutor, was capable of convincingly denying
any evidence—so long as he wasn't confronted with it
in the midst of his lie.

Moral insanity, in the last analysis, is a kind of menda-
cious stupidity. Thus, to annul his dishonorable discharge
from the Marine Corps, which had sanctioned his defection,
Oswald had written to J. B. Connally, governor of Texas, in
January 1962. He claimed he had "gone to the Soviet Union
to live there for a while—just as Ernest Hemingway had
lived in Paris." And he even went so far as to claim that he
had done so with the approval of the American Embassy in

Moscow. That same month he wrote to a Texas senator, and, complaining about the slowness of the Soviet authorities from whom he was awaiting an exit visa, he concludes in his inimitable style, "I urge you, Senator Tower, to bring up the question of the Soviet Union's keeping a U.S. citizen against his will and his express wishes."

Oswald was not unaware that the governor and the senator could get information from the appropriate agencies, and that all his lies, his written claims, might one day compromise him permanently. Nevertheless, he came out with these untruths as if they were legitimate and irresistible weapons, for they express the fictitious side of his personality.

How can this be explained? His own aggressive act never seemed aggressive to him; he regarded the reaction, the defense he provoked, as violence of which he was the innocent victim. He attacks, wounds, betrays, distorts, and lies—but always in legitimate "anticipated" defense. Had he stolen he would have been convinced he was merely recovering what was rightfully his. When lying he was simply protecting himself against people he thought incapable of *not* misunderstanding him and *not* being unjust to him and *not* humiliating him.

Was Oswald already preparing for the assassination when he began using assumed names: Hidell, Hideel, Osborne, Lee? No, and then again yes.

No, because he was dreaming of a political career that would assure him an extraordinary existence and fame. The man who, in "choosing liberty" in Moscow or in preparing his press conferences and political manifestoes, believed he was about to make a striking entry into international politics certainly didn't intend for a moment to commit an assassination.

But until the end of his life, despite his newspapers and pamphlets, Oswald never grasped the meaning of the expres-

sion "political action." He came closest to understanding it
in the summer of 1963 in New Orleans, but then his immense ignorance burst forth. Claiming to have created a
committee with thirty-five members, when in fact he had
done nothing of the sort, did not trouble him, because for
him, the homeless man with no social substance, politics was
merely a semblance, consisting of endlessly multiplied rumors that brought renown, glory, and, ultimately, power to
some. For this rootless young American publicity *created*
reality rather than simply reflecting it. In the last analysis,
public images alone were real to him. If the New York Fair
Play for Cuba Committee published the information that in
Louisiana progressive forces, under the leadership of Alek
Hidell, were meeting regularly to give energetic support to
the Castro movement, this was, politically speaking, the same
as its being true—or so Oswald thought. And it would be
even truer the day Oswald-Hidell would stand up in an international congress to speak as the delegate of these progressive forces.

Oswald could not help being seduced and led astray by
his discovery that in our century only a thin line separates
the nobodies from those V.I.P.s whose slightest gesture reflects and manifests a limitless renown; and that not a day
passes but some very modest person, no different from anyone else, crosses that line—by singing without a voice,
by parading his silliness before a camera, or, Oswald
thought, by "choosing liberty" as an ex-marine might do,
and talking to the whole world by radio from Havana and
unmasking once and for all the hideous face of rapacious,
and warmongering, imperialism. Oswald no doubt would
have ferociously attacked President Kennedy, author of
the October ultimatum. But that wasn't why Oswald-
Hidell killed him.

John F. Kennedy had introduced a new style and a youthful élan to the handling and presentation of affairs of state. Everything seemed to be in his favor: his youth, his physique, his wealth, his father, mother, and brothers, his wife and children. All the media assured constant and favorable coverage to the activities of this family, for in even the most modest homes such news was a welcome satisfaction to an endlessly alert curiosity. People were in the habit of keeping abreast of every detail in the splendid private, social, and political life of three generations of Kennedys.

"I don't believe that one man should have everything at his disposal and another nothing at all." These were the words of a poor wretch, an obscure man named Leon F. Czolgosz, who tried thus to explain why he had killed President William McKinley in 1901.

Oswald was most certainly of the same mind as Czolgosz; he too compared himself with the President of the United States rather than with people more similar to himself, people who worked to secure material stability for their families, in an atmosphere of increasing affluence. When he was working, Oswald never earned more than the federal minimum, and he must have felt inferior even to his neighbors. But when his imagination confronted him with the celebrities of the world—with John F. Kennedy, for example—he believed himself destined to join them in some miraculous future or else to destroy them in a manner that he alone would determine.

"If only they knew that if I felt like . . ." Giuseppe Zangara, a mason, had said this to himself for months on end. Ostensibly a peaceful man, he had made up his mind to kill a President of the United States. The one he had condemned without appeal, Herbert Hoover, never came to Florida, and Zangara feared for his own frail health too much to risk the Washington climate. He patiently suspended his plans and waited for a President, Hoover or his successor, to come to Miami. It was Franklin D. Roosevelt at whom he finally fired five bullets—in vain (though he did kill the mayor of Chicago). Like Czolgosz, Zangara had acted alone and confided in no one.

In point of fact, a man lives with such a monstrous intention as he does with dreams of happiness in an impossible love or the hope for an immense, liberating inheritance. And generally he will never get around to carrying out his plan because the conditions are never quite right, because there is so much to do in preparation —and, finally, because it is much easier to put off an ultimate act till the last possible moment, arousing no one's suspicion, than to expose oneself to certain death.

Possession of his weapons might have been enough for Oswald—he loved having them around and talked about them all the time—and he might have gone on without ever firing at the President or anyone else—or he might have used them on himself or his wife.

The weekend preceding the fatal Friday could just as easily have been a happy one for him, and no one wanted it not to be; it could have been another day that Marina discovered her husband was using an alias in Dallas; the presidential motorcade could just as easily have taken another route and not gone past the Depository. Admittedly Oswald had left for Irving on Thursday evening to get his rifle—and announced as much by talking about curtain rods; but if his wife had made up with him, if his frustrated desires had been appeased, if the night had mitigated his painful feelings of being left out of everything—if, if, if.

If destiny, that practical joker—oh! Rodion Raskolnikov—hadn't sent repairmen to the sixth floor of the building that very day, and if they hadn't moved all the bookcases to the other end of the room, Oswald could not have said to himself that Thursday, "In any case there's no risk in bringing the rifle here, because I can always hide it between the bookcases." And on Friday morning he wouldn't have found everything rearranged, the piled-up bookcases making a perfect cover for anyone in the recess of the corner window. By going there at noon, with the rifle at his right but easy to hide if need be, Oswald had the liberty to make up his mind at the very last moment. If he remained all alone at the window, if the others, especially the repairmen, left the landing to get a better view, if the presidential car drove by slowly enough for him to take aim—*if.*

That enormous act hinged on the confluence of all these circumstances and the banal logic of little things; on all that, but not on East-West antagonism, nor President Kennedy's politics, nor his ultimatum of October 1962, nor the segregation and integration of Negroes—nor on Lee Oswald's opinions and his alleged Marxism. For, finally, he fired because it was so incredibly easy, almost as easy as *not* firing.

But then, *why* did he do it? Merely to leave his mark on history? Possibly. But it was primarily for his own sake that Oswald had to act. One drowns in humiliation only when he is no longer able to escape his self-hatred. If the individual's relationship to himself develops only as a function of his relationship to his environment, it is no less true that after a certain age every individual behaves toward others according to the imperatives of his own character's leitmotifs, according to the fiction that determines the role he plays and makes him interpret other people's actions as if they, too, were merely playing roles assigned by that same fiction.

For his own sake, Oswald had to perform some kind of simple act, as an exorbitant proof that his difference from others lay in his scandalously misunderstood superiority.

Everyone took part in the presidential festival; the event eclipsed everything else, people had talked of nothing else for days on end. And nothing, absolutely nothing would have changed it if Oswald were dead or had never been born. Yet a gesture, the movement of a finger, was enough to ruin the holiday irremediably and to sow panic in that mindlessly excited mass of people. If he only so desired, he, the nobody . . . The gunsight showed him his target—hazy, but precise enough for a hunter's purposes—the man who "had everything at his disposal," whose image had become more and more impossible to escape.

Lee Oswald fired for the reasons indicated above, but for other reasons as well; his act was prodigiously over-determined, like many actions whose causality and finality disturb and irritate us for their insufficient rationality: *iceberg acts.*

He relied on going unsuspected, even in the probable event that the police discovered the rifle had been ordered by A. Hidell; he believed no one would disclose his true identity. But how *could* he believe it? The very same way he could imagine that governors, senators, consuls, *et al.,* would neglect to gather information and would believe anything he told them.

When he left the Book Depository Oswald must have known that he had at least wounded the President, but he was probably afraid to ask questions. He might have spent hours at the movies without receiving news the entire world was feverishly awaiting, of his guilt.

After so many periods of depression and loneliness, every instant that carried him away from his act immersed him deeper in undreamt-of solitude: he alone, of all the inhabitants of the earth, knew that he was the one everyone hated in those hours and that they wanted to wipe him out like a hideous vermin. He took the gun from his room and left.

Should anyone stop him he would shoot instantly, for he had nothing to lose.

He could have turned himself in and arrogantly taken the consequences of his crime; a few minutes later he would have been known throughout the world. But he didn't even admit it when he was interrogated and indicted. To understand his behavior we must survey the relatively unexplored relationship between the man and his actions—and, sometimes, their strange apparent unconnection.

1. Every man is able to act in accordance with a stricturing finality—as if he could remove all the inevitable effects of his act, all but the one he expects. This stricturing characterizes all acts of madness and most crimes of passion: "I absolutely *had* to kill him; I never for one single instant desired his death." Oswald, firing at President Kennedy, wanted to hit the great man and see him, standing in his car, collapse and fall; but he had no reason for wishing him to die.

2. The stricturing finality does not suffice to make a man capable of a crime of passion or a seemingly gratuitous crime. He has to be subject to the *despotism of the present instant,* which prevents him from thinking about what will happen afterward. The illusion of happiness—"Tarry, you moment, you are so beautiful"—is transformed into "Act without fear, there'll be no tomorrow!"

Thus moral insanity inspires "situational" acts whose agents behave as if there were no future and no dire consequences of their terrible deeds. The adolescent who kills the taxi driver in the courtyard of his paternal home, simply to seize his car and meet someone who's not even waiting for him, acts in accordance with that same moral insanity, just as Lee Oswald did in the recess of the window at the moment the motorcade passed by.

3. If it is not unreasonable to judge acts by their direct and (if possible) indirect consequences, it is psychologically indispensable to situate them in relation to their agent, with causes and motives as well as with the final intention that kindles them. Squeezing a trigger is the gesture by which the hunter brings down his prey; the very same gesture kills a President. There is a temptation in the gesture, in the *abstract act;* this temptation draws us all, but irresistibly seduces those without shadows.

Now Oswald was not an assassin per se—not the type of man who had killed Umberto I of Italy, Presidents Sadi Carnot and Paul Doumer, Empress Elizabeth of Austria, and so many others; nor was he the type that had assassinated or tried to kill American Presidents—*e.g.,* Czolgosz and Zangara (mentioned above), or Guiteau, who had murdered James A. Garfield, or John Shrank, who had fired at Theodore Roosevelt. All of them, the anarchists and the others, frighteningly alone, had considered themselves regicides. They acted in full knowledge that there would be no hope of escape; they intended to fulfill themselves in their final acts and, clinging to the body of a chief of state, to leap into glorious oblivion.

None of this applies to Oswald. If the evidence had ultimately crushed him—and it *would* have—he would have confessed, only to hide behind his political clichés. He actually imagined that John Abt would take over his defense and, supported by the Communists and their committees, help him to become the hero of a great cause. He obstinately refused to say anything before consulting with "his" lawyer. Though he would never have obtained Abt's assistance, a good attorney, seconded by psychiatrists, could have managed to save him from the electric chair, as a poor eternal orphan who was not at all what he thought he was, and whose terrible crime was to him merely an abstract act.

I have defined and denounced the *police conception of history* as well as the legend of treason, characteristic of an era depraved and terrorized by fleetingly triumphant totalitarians. The police, I said, does not make history; it merely punctuates an occasional somber episode—usually perversely and illiterately.*

What might be described as the great misery of the political police is the talk and speculation that follow an assassination. Reproaches for their lack of foresight are followed close behind by suspicions that the police instigated the crime and are thus themselves the real culprit. They didn't immediately uncover the conspiracy? Of course not, they themselves are at its nexus. Have they found the culprit so quickly? He must be innocent. Is he killed by an intruder two days later? The man couldn't be innocent—he's an assassin reduced forever to silence by his accomplices.

Except for Abraham Lincoln, assassinated immediately after the close of the Civil War, no American President has ever fallen victim to a plot. And for good reason: In a democratic country the natural or violent demise of a Chief of State involves certain changes of personnel but few political consequences of any real gravity.

On the other hand, if someone had killed Hitler in June 1934, or in November 1939, or in July 1942, his regime would have toppled sooner, the war would have come to a quicker end, and the situation would not have been as desperate as it was in May 1945. And millions of innocent victims who perished in the holocaust of Nazi violence would still be with us. We can even easily imagine the extent to which the Communist movement and the present-day world would be different if someone had taken Lenin's advice and gotten rid of Stalin or killed him the moment when, as abso-

* See "La Conception policière de l'histoire," *Preuves* no. 36, Feb. 1954; and *Le Talon d'Achille*, Editions Calmann-Lévy.

lute master of a totalitarian machine, he became an inexorable liquidator. But the Czolgoszes, the Zangaras, the Gorgouloffs, and others like them almost never attack dictators.

What political result could conspirators hope for after the assassination of President Kennedy? None. They could not help but realize that anyone citing the martyred President and promising faithfully to pursue his policies would have much greater chances in the coming elections. Conspirators should have put everything in gear on November 22, 1963, at 12:30 P.M. and in the following hours, to overthrow the government of the United States of America and to seize all military command posts, as well as administrative, technological, and economic control centers, plus all means of communication. Now, fourteen months after the assassination, we know with absolute certainty that no such thing happened —anywhere in the immense territory of the United States.

But even if there was no conspiracy in the true sense of the word, there may have been an explosion of hate fomented by certain ultra-reactionary circles. Need we recall that the hatred openly nurtured by vested interests toward Franklin D. Roosevelt because of the New Deal was of an entirely different caliber and objectively better founded. Yet there was never a plot against his life.

Actually, hatred acts opportunely against the weak; it works against the strong only after their fall. Hatred easily sets in motion pogromist masses and groups to sully the bodies of the conquered, and seek relaxation in shaving the heads of xenophiliac girls. No, hatred never kills those at the summit of their power; it never caused the death of John F. Kennedy. The Warren Report shows and demonstrates this beyond the shadow of a doubt.

Nevertheless, a considerable number of contemporaries, especially in Europe, prefer to doubt. And not just people who live professionally on rumors and sensational suspicions, but serious and sincere men as well. One of them, the British historian Hugh Trevor-Roper, ferociously attacked the Warren Report, without, however, impressing us as having studied it with the attention it deserves. As a matter of fact, he didn't have to consult it to become a skeptic; long before the Report's publication he was "convinced that the make-up of the Warren Commission and its announced procedure were ill-calculated to produce the truth." * In June 1964 he joined a committee with the interrogative, detective-story title: "Who Killed Kennedy?" We also know that another member of this committee, the formidable, poly-pragmatic nonagenarian Bertrand Russell, goes even further in his offensive skepticism of the Warren Commission.

Lord Russell and his admirers should, however, have been among the first to be grateful for one of the unusual merits of that Commission. Anyone studying the rich biographical documentation on Lee Oswald knows how easy and even tempting it would have been to deduce that the act was fanatically pro-Castroist or perhaps Communist. One might merely re-read † the left-wing British press during the week of the Cuban crisis in 1962, with its attacks on Kennedy and his measures, to be impressed by the fact that the Commission attached no importance to the possibility of a possible detrimental influence on Lee Oswald, who was a diligent reader of newspapers of the same unconditionally pro-Castroist and anti-Kennedy inspiration. And we can't forget that not too long ago Joseph McCarthy's anti-communism dominated public opinion to a fearful degree.

During some twenty-five years, until 1956, the U.S.S.R., with the help of countless organizations at its service, philosophers, scientists, scholars, jurists, writers, journal-

---

* *Sunday Times,* December 13, 1964.
† See *Encounter,* January 1963.

ists, and many others, spread its legend of treason throughout the world. Non-Communist newspapers, too, published articles, eye-witness reports, and studies to the effect that Stalin was infallibly right and the victims of his firing squads and in camps were simply the most ignoble of traitors. During the war an American ambassador, who fancied himself a writer, tried to demonstrate that through these massacres Stalin was saving both Russia and the Allies.

People thus believed that Trotsky was the head of an international conspiracy acting on the orders of Hitler, that Bukharin was in the service of the Japanese police, that Tukhashevski was a *Wehrmacht* spy (all had confessed), and that great Russian doctors of a Jewish background were killing their patients for Zionism.

Is it due to a lasting effect of the Stalinist depravity that certain people find it so difficult to give up the idea of a tenebrous plot against Kennedy? Perhaps. Or is it due to a suspicion of the United States and its institutions, a distrust that the Sacco and Vanzetti case aroused in Europe some forty years ago, and with good reason? Yet the America of the twenties no longer exists; since then the condition of the workers, both as citizens and as members of a class, has changed more than in any other industrial nation. Certainly racist violence is causing revolting complications in certain states, in Mississippi for instance; but distrust and anti-American propaganda won't help in the fight against the racism practiced in the United States.

Nevertheless, skepticism remains useful always and everywhere; one does well to distrust any political police. But one should also be careful not to overestimate its powers, its roles, or its secrets, which in a democratic government are without any great scope.

There is only one secret simultaneously numberless, anodyne, and fearful, and it is one that everyone perceives just as he perceives, yet is unaware of, himself: the secret of human nature, that of Oswald for example.

This American tragedy will be remembered long after scores of others, after many European tragedies.*

* Jack Ruby-Rubinstein, too, is a hero and anti-hero of this tragedy; his case deserves to be studied.

Man and His Deeds

I

"ACTIONS speak louder than words." This well-known cliché is an expression of common sense. We all believe that man expresses himself unequivocally in his actions and not in other ways. We all know that words just as often conceal thoughts and feelings as they reveal them. Each of us believes our essence and our actions are one.

The secret break-up of this unity is the dramatic foundation of conventional detective stories. Famous authors of this literary genre—for example, Sir Arthur Conan Doyle, the father of the infallible Sherlock Holmes—draw their themes from the fact that some people are essentially double-tracked, as it were, and thus able to lead a double life and to appear equally authentic in each of two morally opposed guises. These people manage never to arouse suspicion until finally a Sherlock Holmes sees through them.

The reader of court proceedings is always left with the impression that a crime is something enigmatic. Judges, lawyers, experts of all kinds hunt through the malefactor's life for events, processes and situations to explain, if not justify, the misdeed that no one would have expected of him. The not always trustworthy snooping into the prior life of the defendant; the uninhibited chatter of the witnesses, who claim retroactively to have known something they never really suspected; psychiatric reports that are all too often full of contradictions—all this never actually leads to a satisfying elucidation. Fundamentally, there is no explanation for the fact that this man committed a crime, although we can easily find in any man's life all those elements that might explain, in retrospect, that a misdeed was predetermined, if not made inevitable, by the character, way of life, and personal relations of the delinquent. We are all given to such cheap determinism because we cannot bear any threat to our belief in the unity of personality. Each of us wants to be assured of being a single identity, unchanging and unique.

If, then, the awareness of a basic integrity of personality is essential to man's self-conscious existence, the question of the criminal's relationship to his own sudden act raises alarming doubts as to whether he always, and only, acts in harmony with himself.

It is not only the experts who have to somehow cope with the fact that there may be a flagrant contradiction between the past forty years in the life of a harmless person and the misdeed that he commits in one single moment, to the surprise of all. This moment, and everything resulting from it, throws those forty years into question, since there is no obvious way of deducing the delinquency from them. The misdeed has to be regarded as an inexplicable event if the prior life of the delinquent is to retain its sense, and its structure the normality that no one has hitherto called into question.

Man has always reflected on the nature of his own action —frequently in deep disquiet because of the possibility that an unknown being might dwell within him, a demon who in some unguarded moment might gain control of his senses and his mind and act for or against him.

II

There are more cogent and even tragic reasons for a closer investigation of this problem in our era than in any other time. For in our century great numbers of people have continually repeated unheard-of crimes as if they were merely practicing a profession—without doubting themselves or losing the respect of others. They remained fathers, husbands, brothers, friends—performing as well or as badly as they had before, concerned about the welfare of their family and friends, bothered by the sufferings of their neighbors, perhaps sensitive to poetry and music. They remained all this and yet were incessantly thinking up, organizing, arranging, and carrying out hideous crimes. Thus, whether or not we like it, we, their contemporaries, are faced with a frightening distortion of humanity. We are forced to find some answer to the question: Is there any limit of evil that no man can cross? Is there any limit to man's descent? Are there any deeds that man will not commit at any price? And on the other hand: What sort of personality will not submit to repressive power and will remain unyielding before the seduction of evil?

The first time I asked myself about the relationship of a man to his action was in a situation that was far from ordinary. I was in a group cell of the prison at the main police station in Berlin; it was March 1933. We were in so-called "protective custody"; most of us had been apprehended by the S.A., maltreated, and turned over to the police. Now we lay or stood about, crowded together in the grotesquely stuffed cell, which had to continually absorb more and more prisoners. One evening a young man who had been beaten bloody was dumped into the cell. Other prisoners instantly took care of him, washing his face and giving him something to drink. Upon regaining consciousness, he appeared deeply alarmed. His situation was as grave as that of the other prisoners. He and his wife had been handing out subversive leaflets near their home, and had been caught and arrested.

Since he lay next to me, I became the witness of his insomnia, his tormenting disquiet. He finally summoned up enough courage to speak, and I learned that he was bothered by something other than fear of the consequences of his political action. He had reckoned with these consequences beforehand. But he had bought furniture on the installment plan, and after only two more installments the furniture would belong to him. He was at a loss as to what to do if he and his wife were sentenced to prison and would thus be unable to meet the last two payments. "You understand," he kept on repeating, "if I don't pay the company will take the furniture back and we'll lose everything, and we've pinched and saved for the bedroom and the buffet and the silk couch." This man wasn't unusually bright, but he wasn't at all stupid. He hadn't underestimated the danger to which he and his wife had exposed themselves by handing out leaflets in a popular thoroughfare, leaflets that could be recognized as illegal at first sight. Yet he had gone about it unhesitatingly, true to the political choice he had made beforehand. Not once, however, had he thought about the furniture. He had never once connected it with the possible consequences of his daring action. The furniture and the leaflets were on two different levels. His revolutionary readiness and his petty bourgeois dream of prosperity did not exclude each other simply because they existed in different frames of reference. Their incompatibility became obvious only when he regained consciousness in the cell after his encounter with the S.A. bullies.

I don't know what became of the young man, for two days later I was transferred to solitary confinement. I never saw any of my fellow prisoners again. Yet I am certain that this young man, whom no threat and no maltreatment could force to disloyalty, never yielded and never betrayed his comrades. If he did, then it was only to save the furniture. Naturally it wasn't the money he cared about. He wouldn't have divulged his dangerous secret for millions; but the thought that the precious furniture might be taken away was so unbearable that he may possibly have forgotten his determination against betrayal.

One can draw an important lesson from the case of my cellmate. Even the simplest man acts more or less unconsciously, with different standards according to which he commits or fails to commit actions—usually in such a way as to be ultimately justified. These often incommensurable standards correspond to enclaves in our beings, which one would think are hermetically sealed from one another. The individual psychological unity of the personality is in no wise impaired, but the contradictory variety of the expressive and phenomenal forms can be very surprising, highly dramatic and often confusing.

III

We are faced with a disproportion which, seen from outside, usually remains incomprehensible. We know that in the struggle for a career, a seat of office, a place to park a car, sometimes all means of physical assault are used until murder and manslaughter put a loathsome and senseless end to the fight. Such an act cannot be explained by ambition or possessiveness alone, no matter how greedy the person may be. The greedy are often given to forging, cheating, embezzling; but they very rarely commit acts of annihilation for understandable reasons. Thus, the man on trial for killing a colleague at work in a fight over a pack of cigarettes could swear that he wouldn't harm a fly for the sake of any property. Consequently, the object of the fight was meaningless, simply a pretext in a personality struggle, whose true motives remain unconscious for both parties. When normally functioning inhibitions are gone, violence is given full rein.

And for this very reason, we should make every effort to investigate the circumstances leading to an act of violence.

Thousands and thousands of craftsmen, workers, gardeners, peasants, bookkeepers, engineers, doctors, lawyers—in a word, people whose professions are not connected with any sort of violence—have been ready and willing to routinely degrade, torture, and kill helpless prisoners without feeling the slightest scruple. Were these actions part of their character? Were there elements in their prior life indicating in advance that this dark side of their nature would be hideously revealed in circumstances favoring inhumanity? There is even more reason to pursue the investigation since these imperious myrmidons, these monstrous autocrats of ghettoes and concentration camps, eventually returned home to their wives and children, their bakeries and restaurants, their shops and offices, when everything was over—as if nothing had happened. And the life they have been leading since has never hinted at the crimes they committed day after day for years. They seem to have been on round-trip excursions to hell; wading through the blood of their victims and still managing to keep their feet dry. And, if total oblivion doesn't exist, there is still such a thing as—how shall I put it—the satisfying disactualization of a criminal action that lasted for years. Is this conceivable? If so, what is mankind worth? And what is humaneness worth?

I would like to mention another experience, an encounter. One winter morning in January 1946 in Rastatt I was at a trial that was nearing its end. A French military tribunal was judging the crimes of some twenty-five guards of concentration camps. The defendants, all in civilian clothing, had been in prison for several months. Their faces didn't reveal this; they were made up for the camera, for cameramen had come to film the sentencing for newsreels.

During the final hours of the trial I sat near these men who had committed hideous crimes day after day for a number of years. They had rarely acted in an uncontrolled burst of rage; cruelty had been part of their daily work. It was no use looking away; I couldn't help staring at their miserable, commonplace faces. The red chalk made their features neither more cruel nor more attractive in the powerful lights: the garish lighting simply made their pitifulness weirdly three-dimensional. Everyone who has been imprisoned knows that a long period of incarceration warps the face, making it look as if one deserves one's fate, as if one had been born for it.

I could discover no criminal features in these ordinary, quite often vulgar, yet otherwise unremarkable faces. If I had met any of these men outside, in a subway, a bar, a sports arena, I would never have noticed them.

Yet these men were not indifferent passers-by but true villains of our time, exposed in the glare of the cameras for what they were: exterminators, tyrants who deprived their helpless prisoners of all human rights and then tortured them to death.

We all know that a good number, if not all, of these defendants would be sentenced to death and executed within a few days. I don't want to discuss my own feelings. This wasn't the first time I had been made aware that the defeated enemy of today bears so little resemblance to the triumphant enemy of yesterday that one hesitates to identify the two or make today's enemy responsible for the crimes of yesterday's. And, just a few months after the catastrophe that had lasted five and a half years, it seemed there could be no atonement for the destruction wrought upon the world by these men and their leaders and countless quiet accomplices. I knew that after such a deluge of blood, after such a storm of unhumanity, there could be no revenge and no retribution. Thus I looked into these faces with no desire for revenge but only with infinite amazement and horror that such unsightly creatures could have spent years of daily work being paid for crimes of superdimensional evil.

As a psychologist I had made a habit of regarding every human being as if I might be he and he I, as if I could have committed his crimes, as despicable as they might be. Could I manage to regard the defendants in this way? I wondered this during those minutes in which the uniformed judges prepared to announce, in a tone of indifference, one death sentence after another. Ever since that January morning from which two decades separate me, I have not stopped attempting that experimental identification over and over again—in an unceasing effort to arrive at a full understanding of what has happened to *all* of us in this century. One has to view the malefactor in terms of the deed, and one has to see the deed in its over-all context of contemporary social development, as well as the development and environment of the person himself (all these things being inseparably interlocked).

IV

The crimes of a professional criminal are, relatively, much easier to grasp, one reason being that they are more limited in their conditionality. Criminology and psychiatry explain more or less convincingly why and how someone becomes a professional criminal with little conscience or feeling. These psychological defects used to be known as "moral insanity." This term referred primarily to the incurable incapacity of a criminal to resist the lure of crime or to regard his own actions in terms of any moral law or social demand —that is to say, critically. Thus the professional criminal is unable to live without constantly breaking some law. On the other hand, the violence we have been speaking of has nothing to do with "moral insanity" or professional criminality;

it is connected with supra-individual facts, with society and politics. A war turns any soldier into a potential murderer or, if you prefer, slaughterer. In both world wars, millions of men planned and carried out annihilation for hours, days, and months. Everyone knows that, except for a few rare cases, soldiers are not bothered by conscience after firing at human beings on command, destroying fields and forests, razing houses and whole cities, and devastating everything that makes the lives of others easier. Should we see a connection between the ruthless murderers of concentration and extermination camps and the man-hunters and destroyers into which decent people are transformed by the laws of their countries from one day to the next? Granted there have always been wars, and they have always been accepted by people, like hail by the farmer; and there may even be a purely psychological explanation for the fact that military destruction—for example the bombing of a city—weighs less heavily on the conscience of the destroyer than a knifing on the conscience of a criminal. The latter's nearness to the victim, their physical contact, makes the act personal and, in a certain sense, corresponds to the archetypal fratricide committed by Cain. But the throwing of a bomb, the firing of artillery, or the cross-fire aimed at a storm of enemies has something anonymous and therefore impersonal about it.

This distinction is well-founded, but we must not forget the possibility of close fighting, a surprise attack, hand-to-hand fighting for one's life. In this situation, however, every soldier may think that he is acting in legitimate defense, that he must kill before his opponents kills him. The argument of self-defense has therefore always played a great part in unleashing wars and in military propaganda. Politicans have always made a great effort to give their nations a feeling of moral justification by persuading them they were compelled to defend themselves against a wicked enemy.

Almost *every* spontaneous act of violence is probably sparked by the feeling that one is acting or has to act in self-defense; i.e., by a more or less conscious, usually inadmissible fear. Thus sadism, for example, within and beyond sexuality, is quite obviously the result of a boundless fear of losing one's will-power, of being raped and ultimately destroyed. This fear is accompanied by a total or partial impotence, and by the inability to love or express love in any other way than by suppressing or degrading the partner.

V

It may be, however, that neither psychology nor psychopathology suffices to explain the actions we are talking about here, simply because those disciplines are inadequate in the face of a problem that is essentially philosophical rather than psychological. For we can claim that the gist of the problem involving the relationship of man to his own actions is the fact that an action is seldom limited in its effect to the extent that the malefactor intends or anticipates. There is sometimes a fatal discrepancy between the purpose of the action and the other effects, which are usually unpredictable and certainly uncalculated. These effects may be seen as side effects from the viewpoint of the malefactor. Yet frequently they become the main effects, since the consequences can be immeasurable. This main problem is actually linked to the fatefulness of every tragedy. For the tragic would not exist without two crucial elements: the unattained goal of the protagonist, *and* the unpredictable consequences of his action.

On the one hand we need only think of the quite trivial yet ultimately fatal action of the housewife who carelessly drops a heavy object from her windowsill just as a child passes by; the child is mortally struck and dies. What is such an act? Without the lethal effect due to the dreadful coincidence, it is merely a careless movement of the hand, the usual consequence of which is some damaged object. The terrible effect, which so-called chance brings about, has no connection with the essential character of the woman, her intentions, or her mode of life. She is as much an object as her victim.

But in the tragic theater, which condenses and dramatizes the fatality of our actions, the process is different and therefore far more revealing. For the warning is stated and frequently reiterated long before the action is carried out. Everyone learns that something terrible is going to happen but that fate can still be averted. Yet the warnings either have no effect or, if taken seriously, drive the threatened people to commit the very deeds they should have avoided at any price. King Laius is warned that his own son will kill him. Consequently, he wants to kill the male child that is born to him, for he is convinced that he can thus elude the fate prophesied for him. But by so doing he makes possible the events that eventually lead to his death. Oedipus will kill Laius without recognizing him as his own father. The knowledge of destinies is useless if it does not open the eyes of the threatened man to the scope of the actions with which he hopes to escape destiny. Oedipus would never have killed his father if he had known him; he would never have married his mother if she hadn't deliberately severed the bond with her own child and rejected maternity. Thus every true tragedy reveals our self-estrangement through the estrangement of the purpose of our actions and thereby the fateful incongruity between intention and result.

My teacher Alfred Adler, the founder of individual psychology, used to make fun of the critics who chided Hamlet for his "procrastinating attitude." Adler would say: "I'd like to see the theater critic who'd kill his uncle and plunge his mother into grief just like that." Adler thus jestingly re-

jected the apparently profound but actually shallow inter-
pretation of Shakespeare's tragedy in terms of the young
prince's supposed incestuous relationship to his mother and
his Oedipus complex with regard to his uncle. This example
once again makes clear how wrong psychology can be when
it tries to attribute a fundamentally philosophical situation
to the psychological accidents of childhood. Hamlet's pro-
crastination is in accordance with the philosophical mind
that realizes that an action cannot be isolated, that it can involve undesired and unanticipated effects—in short, that *the
doer no longer controls the deed once he has committed it.*
The accomplished act repudiates him and his goals, moves
away from him, and has greater and greater consequences.
Thus the doer resembles a man who, in order to find a road
in the darkness, ignites a fire that causes an explosion whose
end he will not live to see. It was this realization, and not
what Nietzsche termed "a procrastinating attitude," that
caused Hamlet's timidity. And Hamlet was right. Not only
did the guilt-ridden king die, but also Ophelia and Hamlet
himself and Laertes and so many others whose death the
prince never desired. The frightening disproportion between the above-mentioned "sloppy gesture" of a housewife
and the death that results threatens us all in our daily actions. However, if we remained aware of this constantly
and tried to act accordingly we would escape one danger
only to fall victim to another, no less dangerous, one: we
would shrink from any action. We would come to a stand-
still which would endanger our existence and deprive it
of all meaning.

VI

This is one aspect, both tragic and comic, of the wide divergence between intention and result, action and effect.

There is, however, another aspect, without which the history of mankind would have been quite different, without which the concept of leading characters, the Hegelian "world-historical personalities," could not exist. One need merely inspect the biography of a successful statesman, a general, or a revolutionary. Naturally historians prefer describing the lives of those who have "made it"; they illuminate only those who already stand in a flattering light. Let us examine the case of the Bolshevik leader Lenin. A few months before the uprising began in Russia, Lenin declared in his Swiss exile that he believed in the Revolution but that it would only come much later, after his death. If he had actually died at that point, at the age of forty-six, then everything he had accomplished in the course of his life would have been essentially inconsequential. He had shaped a faction into a party that never stopped dissipating its energy in factional fighting; he had written a good number of things that rarely had the desired effect, as well as sharp polemics that quickly lost their topicality, and countless articles that were no worse but usually no better than those authored by his fellow revolutionaries. No one would ever have dreamed of publishing these writings as collected works. Then came the revolution that got rid of the Tsar; Lenin and his comrades played almost no part in it. They had neither prepared for it nor anticipated it in time. But then there followed actions of decisive importance, which proved that Lenin had enormous political intelligence, energy, and courage, as well as a sense for and a will to power.

He died six years and two months after the establishment of the Soviet Republic and only two years after the termination of the Civil War, during which time his power was continuously shaky. In his final years Lenin was tormented by growing doubts as to whether the thing he had helped to create was good, by fears that it was heading irresistibly in a direction opposed to his wishes. Until the very last moment, this exemplary victor was afraid that his victory might be spoiled and his life's goal unattained.

Now everything that has since been written about Lenin —by admirers or enemies—has been written in the light of his triumph. His various initiatives, his articles, his countless polemics, his unconvincing, badly grounded philosophical writings—all this has been presented during the last forty years as highly original and historically important. And only because it is connected not with his original positions and limited goals but with the power of the heirs who invoke him and his doctrine. Everything is always presented as if Lenin had foreseen and carefully planned everything that subsequently happened; for example, the tyranny of Stalin, whom he despised.

Thus most biographies of successful men involve the *re-interpretation of facts in terms of a postulated congruence of intention and result,* which in reality was rarely if ever achieved.

In all such cases, there is, if I may call it that, a *systematic magnification,* a magnification by multiplication. A larger or smaller coefficient is used to magnify a world-historical personality or a lesser luminary. In every case, the historian falsifies the perspectives and covers up the disproportion. As the French say, one lends only to the rich.

We are actually faced with a double disproportion. On the one hand we are unable to foresee all the ultimate results of even banal actions, much less to prevent them; on the other hand we tend to see an action as immeasurably magnified if it is carried out by a man who seems important for any reason whatsoever. Frequently one even applies this process of falsification retroactively. This is something that those very popular and bad biographers do who see all the indications of later greatness in the very childhood of their hero.

VII

Are we unable to correctly judge the apparently most unequivocal expression of our essence: the act? Are we doomed to remain naïve and trusting toward our own actions if we are not constrained from acting by Hamlet's doubts? If these questions are appropriate in regard to our everyday acts within our families, in our work, with our friends, our actions become even more problematical when we realize that not only may their subsequent effects be alien to us but they may sometimes alienate us from ourselves. We may discover, in acting, that we are not—or not only—what we think we are because we suddenly discover in ourselves the features of a being unknown to us beforehand. This is true of behavior which initially seems totally innocuous and insignificant, grows important under specific circumstances, and finally determines our life for a shorter or longer period. It forces us in a direction we would never take if we were capable of foretelling the final issue. This would be a case of *individual change* as *mass phenomenon,* a frequent occurrence in our century and in past eras as well; for example, in connection with religious wars.

Countless people have joined movements which at first demanded only consent to a general political philosophy or simply a hazy idea of the world. Most of them believed that their position would remain more or less without consequences. They were ready to vote for the Party and applaud its speakers, but only on the periphery of their private life, and they thought it would remain there. The political activity brought some welcome diversion into everyday life and gave the feeling of being in harmony with other people and

with a whole movement. A person might fill out a question-
naire, become a card-carrying member, and pay the (at least
initially) moderate dues. One's relations at home and with
one's friends, at work and during vacations, were not
touched. But the greater the conflicts between the competing
movements became, and the more ferocious the struggle for
power, the deeper and more demanding politics became in
one's private life. One could no longer refrain from conflicts
with diverging opinions; the result was often fighting and ultimately the rupture of relationships that had been safe because they were psychologically comfortable. It was like a
triumph of logic, the *logic of struggle,* as the Communists
and so many extremist movements after them termed the disastrous concatenation of positions, commitments, and dichot-
omizing conflicts. The final result was extremism in politics
and in the everyday life of each individual.

We must not forget that there is such a thing as a virtually
solitary, or private, extremism. We produce it ourselves. It
corresponds to the seasons of our life and changes that come
along with them. There is the highly peculiar, still uninves-
tigated extremism of childhood, often manifest in feeble cruelty. We know the extremism of youth, the most natural and
certainly the most sensible. One cannot grow up without
brutally breaking with a great deal of what one has grown
up with and through. For in these difficult years of development one has to go a long distance away from one's first
teachers in order to become certain of getting along without
them. One has to smash the mold that holds the formed
work captive. The frequently confusing, passionate friendships of young people are often leagues against a world by
which they feel inadequately recognized, and therefore misunderstood and repressed.

The usual adult mode of life is unfavorable to the contin-
uance of these friendships; the establishment of a family

seems to make them superfluous, the tempered climate of everyday living destroys extremisms of any sort; they are often replaced by harmless hobbies. The adult tries to create *stable* conditions to which he can adjust by means of *psychic automatisms.*

In view of this state of affairs, one may claim that the first few weeks of war or a fanatical movement may offer enthusiasts something like rejuvenation, an illusory return to a lost youth. The stodgy routine of daily actions, words and phrases, of almost unchangeable relations and habits, becomes questionable if not suddenly invalid. As provoking as it may seem, despite all its horrors, war means, above all, a long vacation for the soldiers—a vacation from everyday life, marriage, invariable work, as well as a welcome escape from an unchanging neighborhood and one's home and friends. In short, it is an abrogation of secure standards and the corresponding actions and behavior. War stabilizes, as it were, extreme situations, which, by definition, cannot be stable; and it forces into existence an extremism of action and— albeit temporarily—of feelings and opinions.

The fanatical mass movements of our time intrude into situations that are not extreme in any way, and transform everyday people, careful heads of families as well as frivolous adolescents, into extremists with an increasing need to repulse and even annihilate anyone not in total accordance with them; and vice versa, they feel at one with all those with whom they share a boundless admiration for leaders, extreme political ideas, and especially a common enemy.

VIII

The permanent invasion of one's private sphere will not infrequently force out the rule of loyalty which normally governs personal life. A hitherto unknown disorder will spread, for whatever the individual is henceforth ready to do has little connection with his psychic automatisms or, more generally, with his previous life. He may previously have been a decent person, but he will not hesitate to carry out indecent, disloyal, even treacherous actions if the cause seems to warrant it, and—this is decisive—his conscience will remain as deaf as that of a "morally insane" criminal. He will not only not feel debased, but will actually find satisfaction in what he considers his "self-expansion," the magnification of his personality, and the certitude of attaining to greater importance. He will speedily be convinced that the more treacherously he behaves the more loyal he is—like Hagen in the Nibelungen Saga, who cunningly gains Kriemhild's and Siegfried's confidence and betrays Siegfried's secret in order to murder him. It may, incidentally, be revealing to note that this dubious hero has always been acclaimed in German textbooks as the epitome of loyalty because of his willingness to commit any infamy for his master Gunther. Loyalty proven by betrayal, treachery in the name of loyalty, as it were, is extremely characteristic of the attitude that fanatic movements demand of their followers. To make such an inversion of values succeed, the fundamental rules of decency in social intercourse have to be abolished.

Thus we return to the question of standards with which we, consciously or unconsciously, knowingly or unknowingly, determine our behavior. Thanks to these practical criteria, people feel they can tell the exact difference between good and evil. They act in the certainty that it is more sensible and more useful to do good than evil, to create rather than damage, to build rather than destroy. But in such normal situations, the road is clearly marked; one never leaves it without good reason. We are never tested and we never want to be tested. The individual has to mobilize neither his will power, nor his capacity to doubt anything, nor any sort of enthusiasm. Only when we enter extreme situations—through personal conflicts or under the pressure of contemporary events—are we really put to test. It is actually a matter of luck. People are lucky who have lived during periods of gradual and peaceful change, and who have consequently had no need to prove themselves beyond their normal capabilities or to exhibit great courage against seductive or extortionate evil. But we are speaking here amid the ruins of castles in the air and as heirs to utopias run amuck. We are dealing with the problem of the relationship between man and action in a period in which extreme situations have abolished or completely changed everyday life over and over again and for years at a time, for hundreds of millions of people. And we have to ask ourselves how these people stood the test.

What should our standards be? If, for example, one allows one's nation an absolute privilege, i.e., grants that everything is lawful that serves the interests of one's own people, then what general principles will remain valid? None at all! If there is no universally binding law then the individual no longer has the ability to decide between good and evil, loyalty and treason, duty and freedom. The age of pre-adulthood, of "pupilage," will be upon us, the age about which Kant said the following:

"Pupilage is the inability to use one's own mind without the guidance of someone else. Such pupilage is self-afflicted if caused not so much by a lack of intelligence as the lack of resolution and courage to use one's intelligence without someone else's guidance." Immanuel Kant wrote these words in his work on the Enlightenment, nearly 150 years before Hitler's victory over Germany and Stalin's victory over communism.

In a state of pupilage, every function becomes a highly valued service. The servants, however, have an easy time of it, for they have no qualms to overcome and it is not up to them to choose a goal. They don't have to ask their consciences or answer to them. The obsequious and the servile need do only one thing: obey. They will do the most iniquitous deed if ordered to, and when called to account for it afterwards, will have the same answer and the same lack of responsibility: "We were ordered to do it and we obeyed. That was our urgency," they will say, "for if we had acted contrary to orders we would have become victims ourselves."

In a condition of self-afflicted, beatifying pupilage, tens of thousands, countless people, acted for years as if they could autocratically decide on the life and death of completely defenseless victims. They were totally ruthless, they refused their victims any grace; their service was degradation, torture, and murder. We live among them now, or they among us, and we act as if it had all flowed away like water down a river. The crimes are orphaned, so to speak; they have no perpetrators, and never had any to begin with.

Our whole existence is based on mutual trust. When I walk down a street, I practice this trust in a thousand different ways. Someone might attack me from behind or run me down in a car, injure me, kill me. But, sensibly enough, we live in accordance with a probability that has become a certainty—the probability that no one will break the rules of our social contract without a special, recognizable reason. Thus there exists a certain self-control determined by a sense of living in a community and on the basis of a well-understood interest. This self-control does not always guide our actions but it does set certain limits. Civilized people will always live by the rule of doing unto others as they would have them do in return.

It is only in extreme situations that this rule is tested. Action no longer reflects the essence of the perpetrator; to a certain extent, it becomes independent of him. Very often it even starts to react on him and dominate him. Anyone who has acted immoderately—say, committed a murder—will thereafter be dominated in all his actions by that act. He will do anything he can to wipe out all clues, to flee, and nevertheless he will remain under the control of that act. A whole new existence will begin for him.

IX

To sum up, we can state: first, that an act can reach through its consequences beyond anything that the doer intends or even anticipates. This holds particularly for the tragic act committed on the basis of a warning to ward off a disastrous fate. Secondly, there is the magnified act, considered not, as is necessary, in connection with causes, reasons, motives, but in the limelight in which the doer is placed after a great success. Thirdly, there are acts which seem to best correspond to extreme situations, because their immensity cannot be reckoned by any humane standards.

The result of the latter is either the utmost isolation of the perpetrator, or else the massing, the strengthening of a kind of community of accomplices, each member finding glory and justification for his own crimes in those of the other members. Nevertheless, it would be a mistake to believe that extreme situations favor only crime and treason. Anyone trying to understand the events of World War II with some objectivity and with consideration of all the aspects has to realize that no small number of people exceeded themselves in decency, in selfless solidarity, tirelessly ready to save a victim of persecution, genuinely faithful to ideas involving no advantages, no power.

That too is part of extreme situations; that miracle of humanity has frequently emerged in the superdimensional moral catastrophes of our century.

One understands little about people if one fails to realize what they are capable of when overcoming fears for themselves. It is true that they often fail to realize it themselves. This failure is connected with the fact that their self-conceptions do not wholly belong to them—sometimes as little as the immense act belongs to them. The ideal one would like to live up to has been formed since childhood of a curious, mostly obscure mixture of infant fears and exaggerated expectations, inadmissable demands on life and hopes one boldly aspires to only in great moments. All this is mingled in a mass of distorted merging images in which one's reality and ideal are soldered into a monstrous creature that can never exist but that never stops functioning psychologically as if some day it might.

Does a man act as he is or as if he were someone he would like to be? Or in order to avoid being taken for someone he wouldn't like to be but fears he is? Is the deed intended to expand the perpetrator, to magnify his location in reality, or vice versa, to make it seem as if the perpetrator is expressed most truly in the deed, whereas it actually doesn't reveal him so much as disguise him? Is the deed thus a camouflage, a second projected form of Being: an inauthentic, untrue Being?

The answer may be yes or no. For the question of genuineness is infinitely more dfficult than people generally think, especially when it involves the true nature of man. For example, what is a pose? Something inauthentic, of course, a gesture or an action meant to pretend something. But that's not quite true, for the pose, albeit not the *direct* expression of the poseur's character, is nevertheless an *indirect* and certainly authentic expression of his dominant tendency, i.e., his personality ideal and his style of life. The image one would like to create of oneself is as much a part of one's character as appearance is part of reality. Furthermore, an exposed lie reveals more about the liar than any of the trivial truths we normally stuff our conversations with. A lie is a product of so-called *private* intelligence: *a lie is intimate.* The pose in which one believes oneself most likable is the pose in which one likes oneself best. If one fools other people it is only because one is fooling oneself.

Poses are primarily imitations of admired attitudes. A young man carried away by a stage performance will find it hard to resist the temptation to imitate, almost unconsciously, the intonation and the characteristic gesture of the hero he has identified with for an entire evening. All this belongs of course to the changing phases of our youth. We should not forget that we have taken over every word from other people, copied everything from others, for we start out as camels (to quote Nietzsche) who, lacking any sense of discrimination, devour everything that comes our way.

But there were times when a pose was indispensable if one wanted to live up to the aesthetic demands that good society made on the younger generation. Young people posed —and it wasn't always easy. They had to be interesting, e.g., appear to be sick and delicate and what not. Furthermore, they had to think up original ideas, prepare them thoroughly and then "improvise." One example was the practical joke, which greatly amused serious people like Goethe, although it could often be destructive, and even dangerous for outsiders. The so-called "sons of the Muses" were expected to reveal visible signs of their calling. For several decades, Europe admired blatant melancholy as a proof of deep feeling and "high ideality," as people termed it. Has this situation really changed?

We see daily examples of how young people are outwardly influenced by movies and television; in their frenzy to be original, they imitate. The triumph of a movie star results in her laboriously composed replica appearing in countless copies on the streets and dance floors.

Is a pose an act? Or merely a surrogate for an act?

I know of a high-school student who risked his life for the sake of a pose. He had been promoted, and he suffered from the fact that his new classmates didn't pay enough attention to him. To gain their attention he claimed to be an unusually good swimmer. Spring came, they went swimming and he had to offer proof of his prowess. Not courageous enough to tell his schoolmates that he couldn't swim, he exhibited the strange, *cowardly daring of a poseur:* he leaped into the water from the highest diving board. He could have died, but he survived—a cripple forever.

Dangerous poses of that sort are hardly ever kept up to the point of an acid test, but in our time the tendency to costly self-enhancement, which we could term *lying with the truth,* is growing. So-called mass culture is creating a need in previously disadvantaged strata, the petty bourgeoisie and the working class, to acquire blatant marks of prosperity; i.e., apparently unlimited conspicuous consumption. There is a certain correspondence between purposeless independent action and the enslaving pose of luxury now predominant in the people. This pose too is in a way genuine, for it corresponds more than any other modern phenomenon to the widely held belief that happiness lies in the irresistible advance of material progress. In the course of a single generation this advance has totally altered the life-style of a growing number of working people. The ownership of superfluous commodities, surpassing the traditional prestige of luxury, has attained a value that invests objects with new, symbolic meaning.

X

There have been societies of Being, in which the value of a person was determined by his birth. Then came middle-class society, which tried to replace Being with Having. In the aristocratic world of Being and the bourgeois world of Having, work was more or less openly scorned as a proof of poverty and of not belonging. It was industrial society that made work respectable and, in the name of socialism, fidelity to one's work, and general progress, substituted action for Being and Having as a source of value and respect. It is all the more remarkable that, nevertheless, only the *superfluous* act—for example, the athletic feat of a champion—is generally admired; otherwise a Being, whose glow is created by conspicuous Having and the luxury of the superfluous, hogs the limelight. Here, too, the movie star, once a poor, inconspicuous girl, is an example.

But what does all this have to do with the relationship of man and act? Well, perhaps we can draw a lesson from the immediate proximity of extremist periods filled with over-valued deeds, periods followed by a time, *our* time, in which young people feel they can find freedom in aimlessness and indolence and make freedom visible in the conspicuousness of external appearance. This stupendous succession of eras preceding our own leads one to believe that young people have lost all trust in acts, especially great ones, simply because their parents have lived through times that were too great. Great times are usually followed—as in France after the Napoleonic Era—by a devaluation of lofty goals and world-changing undertakings and by a lessening of man's confidence in himself and his calling to transform the world.

The word "act" is unequivocal in appearance only; this syllable can be understood in many different ways. Thus we have spoken about a good number of things but not about the most universal and rarest action, the most fruitful and therefore most important: love, which does more to hold the world together than hunger. In love man's essence may express itself with the greatest variety and frequently in a pose, yet it expresses itself most authentically—even if the lovers initially meet one another in their Sunday best as it were.

As with extreme situations, man seeks to conquer everyday life with love. But only love drives him on to acts in which he doesn't have to lose himself; only in these acts can he discover himself.

About the Author

Manès Sperber was born in 1905 in ancient Austria. A disciple of Alfred Adler, at the age of twenty-one he wrote the first biography of that great psychologist. Dr. Sperber taught psychology in Berlin until he sought exile in Paris, where he now lives as a French citizen. He is one of Europe's most distinguished novelists, essayists, and critics, an editor with Calmann-Lévy in Paris and with Kiepenheuer & Witsch in Germany, and a member of the Board of the International Council of Culture. He has written three novels, *The Burned Bramble, The Abyss,* and *Journey without End,* and a previous volume of essays, *The Achilles Heel.* Dr. Sperber's literary influence and his reputation as humanist and man of letters are highly valued in Europe and increase in this country. He is a frequent reviewer for the *New York Times Book Review.*